Understanding Suffering

UNDERSTANDING SUFFERING

by
B. W. Woods

BAKER BOOK HOUSE
Grand Rapids, Michigan

Copyright 1974 by Baker Book House Company, Inc.

ISBN: 0-8010-9551-4

Quotations from The Amplified Bible, Old Testament. Copyright 1962, 1964. By Zondervan Publishing House and is used by permission.

Quotations from The New Testament in the Language of the People, by Charles B. Williams. Copyright 1966. Moody Press, Moody Bible Institute of Chicago. Used by permission.

Printed in the United States of America

In Memory of Janie
and the radiant faith with which she,
in the morning of her life and amidst the throes of an
incurable illness, bade farewell to her husband
and two small children.

Contents

Foreword 9
Acknowledgments 11

Part One
PERSPECTIVES ON SUFFERING

1 The Non-Christian Perspective 15
2 The Christian Perspective 23

Part Two
CAUSES OF SUFFERING

3 Impersonal Causes for Suffering 33
4 Divine Chastisement 42

Part Three
THE ROLE OF SUFFERING

5 Suffering As Education 53
6 Suffering That Contributes to Spiritual Growth 66
7 Suffering That Proves the Reality of Faith 77
8 Suffering That Reveals God 85
9 Suffering That Teaches Reverence for Life 94
10 Suffering for the Benefit of Others 101
11 Suffering Without Reason 113

Part Four
POWER FOR SUFFERING

12 The Heavenly Father's Love: Love That Lasts 125
13 The Presence of the Living Christ 137
14 The Certainty of Divine Providence: What Do We Need to Fear? 146
15 The Christian View of Death 158
16 The Promises of Heaven 167

Foreword

The most persistent problem facing a Christian is suffering. Where are the books which combine theoretical with practical help? They are difficult to find. To meet this need, B. W. Woods has written this book. *Understanding Suffering* has a number of noteworthy characteristics.

It *combines profundity and clarity*. Well trained, with an earned doctorate in theology, Dr. Woods has forged this material on the anvil of a successful lay and youth ministry. It will challenge the good student but also be helpful for laymen and young people and busy pastors.

The book is based on basic Biblical doctrines and is practical. Christianity can help explain suffering. Dr. Woods has given these basic explanations in a clear and helpful manner. There are strong doctrinal sections in the book dealing with such doctrines as heaven, death, and Satan. The genius of Christianity, however, is the practical help it gives in the midst of suffering. This book reflects this emphasis. Part Three, with six chapters, discusses the role of suffering. Part Four, with five chapters, discusses power for suffering.

The book provides thoughtful and helpful exegesis of the Biblical passages dealing with suffering. There is a discussion of Paul's references to suffering, Hosea, Isaiah 53, Job, I John and many other books and passages. Biblical characters are analyzed from the perspective of suffering. Pastors, Sunday school teachers, and Bible groups will find this material especially relevant to their needs.

Stories coming from actual life experiences are combined with a rich store of material from literature, poetry, philosophy, and contemporary psychologists. This should be especially helpful for Christians who seek to share revealed Biblical truth with non-Christians.

As a theological student, Dr. Woods became deeply interested in the problem of suffering. Since that time, he has become a proven writer and a widely recognized pastor of large churches. He is known as an Evangelical Christian apologist. He has developed a direct, frank, and refreshing literary style. He has a sensitive, devotional touch. All of these elements have resulted in a delightful and stimulating book.

John P. Newport
Professor of Philosophy of Religion
Southwestern Baptist Theological Seminary
Fort Worth, Texas

Acknowledgments

To give credit to everyone who has in some way contributed to the writing of this book is impossible. Footnotes are at best a very limited expression of acknowledgment, for who can trace the influence of others upon one's thoughts?

However, I must pay special tribute to Dr. John Newport, Professor of Philosophy of Religion at Southwestern Baptist Theological Seminary, who first quickened my interest in the problems of evil and suffering and introduced me to the Christian framework within which these problems must somehow be reconciled. I am therefore honored that he should write the foreword to this book.

I must also pay tribute to the members of the congregations who have called me "pastor" and who have taught me much about the kind of faith that can face trials. I think of E. D. Roark and his courageous struggle with a terminal kidney disease; of Wanda Morris who bravely battled leukemia; of Dr. Hugh Simpson whose faith and Christian witness amidst abdominal cancer shone as a light in the darkness.

I think of my niece, Janie Buckwald, to whose memory this book is dedicated, who in her midtwenties quietly fought the ever encircling tentacles of lupus with its fatal complications, and yet kept her zeal for the Lord's work, functioned as an affectionate wife and mother, and died with the dignity of one whose destiny was not dimmed by death.

These, and countless others that cannot be mentioned for lack of space, have touched and blessed my life, and given me a deepened insight into the arena of tears where sooner or later every one of us must do battle.

And last of all a special note of appreciation is due

Mrs. Lou Ann Tyner for her tireless efforts in typing the manuscript, and to my wife, Ann, whose love and encouragement made the book possible.

B. W. Woods
First Baptist Church
Muskogee, Oklahoma

Part One
PERSPECTIVES ON SUFFERING

1

The Non-Christian Perspective

"Why did this happen to me?" The question came from a bewildered mother who blurted it out between sobs. Her son had been killed on the battlefield and the news of it had just arrived.

"There never was a better woman than my wife; why does she have to have leukemia?" The words came from a heartbroken husband upon returning from the office of a specialist.

Each incident, with slight variations, is multiplied hundreds of times each day all over the world. Each instance is a grim reminder that suffering is no respecter of persons. Job is the classic example of a man who wrestled with the problem of suffering.

The philosophical problem of evil was classicly presented by Epicurus three hundred years before Christ: Either God desires to prevent evil but cannot (in which case He is not all-powerful); or He has the power to prevent evil and does not want to (in which case He is not good); or He has neither the power nor the desire to prevent evil (in which case He is neither good nor all-powerful); or He has the power to prevent evil, and wants to (in which case there can be no reason for the presence of evil).

John Stuart Mill has summarized Epicurus and voiced the heart cries of many by saying that God is not both good and all-powerful or He would prevent evil and suffering.

Yet the Christian maintains that God is both good and all-powerful. Before examining the Christian perspective, however, let us look at the futility of any other meaningful answer. Those who are cynical about the

Christian perspective on suffering will do well to see the poverty of any other approach. Those who would disdain all such philosophical quests have failed to see that the predominance of suffering all about forces such a quest for all who would propose to grapple seriously with life, for we shall all suffer.

When Albert Schweitzer died, the *New York Times* devoted a long article to his life accomplishments. Yet out of all his writings and statements, the newspaper quoted only one remark: "Every man must learn to bear his share of the suffering of the world."

Suffering may delay its coming like the slowly gathering summer storm, but sooner or later the pent-up fury sweeps across the horizon and descends on every home. It is well to determine ahead of time the attitude with which the storm is to be endured. A look at the non-Christian answers to suffering will help bring an appreciation for the Word that comes from God.

ATHEISM

Atheism sees suffering as another proof in its portfolio that life and history are meaningless. The story of man is like "a set of tracks made by a drunken fly with feet wet with ink, staggering across a piece of white paper." Any attempt to formulate a meaningful outlook on life is like "a blind man in a dark room searching for a black cat that isn't there."[1] Atheism has nothing to offer to those in the throes of suffering except to say that the sufferer merely bolsters its argument—an argument which, if won, would only bring a reward of utter emptiness. In his attempt to live without recourse to God by denying His existence, the atheist creates a much greater problem than that of suffering. He is left with the problem of how his own personality and rationality could have ever arisen in an impersonal and irrational world.

Existentialism—Perhaps the most popular form of atheism is that of the existential atheists of whom Jean Paul Sartre is representative. One glimpses the emptiness of his world view in his work, *No Exit*. He depicts hell as a place with no opportunity to leave, or to start anew. All things are fixed. Even the eyelids can't blink. Although one of his characters says, "Hell is other people," it is quite apparent that Sartre sees all of life as hell.

Albert Camus, another existentialist, shared with Sartre the belief that man had to be his own center, since the world had none. However, he became disenchanted with his world devoid of values and purpose. The last few moments of his life were spent in a community of Huguenots, a Protestant communion with Calvinistic roots. What he once called "an invincible summer" within him apparently was not enough. His untimely death no doubt prevented his writing about the experience, but it would seem his atheism had offered no real solutions.[2]

Communism.—By far the largest camp of atheism is to be found today in communism. How pathetic that so much of the world's population is in the clutches of a philosophy that makes no attempt to struggle with the sobs of the heart.

Neither Marx, Engels, nor any later Marxists have produced any systematic work on suffering. They have chosen to remain blind to death's grief and sorrow's despair. They concern themselves only with social evils that can be remedied by, they think, social and political organizations. Evil is any attempt to frustrate the purposes of communism. What a cold hope with which to follow a coffin to the cemetery.

ESCAPISM

Another non-Christian category is that which I choose to label "Escapism." The various philosophies within this group do not deny God, but rather seek in one way or another to escape the problem of suffering.

Eastern religions—Eastern religions make little attempt to deal with evil. Typical of their approach is the Islamic expression "in 'shallah," meaning "if Allah wills." Therefore they leave the science of medicine, the building of hospitals, and the problem of suffering up to Allah.

Other Eastern religions, while basically denying the reality of evil, go on to explain that the presence of suffering is the result of wrongs committed in a prior existence. The only answer is to try by good works to be reincarnated in an ever higher existence until at last one can escape the cycle of life and find oblivion through union with the great world principle.

Christian Science —Christian Science, Hinduism, and Buddhism are very similar in their basic denial of evil, though Christian Science is perhaps more total in that denial. Mrs. Eddy taught that God is all; that God is good; that good is mind. Therefore matter is illusory, God and Spirit being all in all. Such belief leads to the denial of death, sin, disease, and evil. The solution to the problem of suffering is the power of the mind to discard the belief that pain and disease exist—the power of mind over matter (nonexistent matter).

Hedonism —Hedonism is a broad term used to encompass all theories that see pleasure as the ultimate goal of life and criterion for conduct. Anything that is fun is good. Anything that is not fun is bad and should be avoided. Playboyism is the most current example of hedonism.

The Playboys of the world overlook the fact that happiness cannot be captured by onslaught. It can only come as a by-product of the responsible, purposeful life. Those who madly pursue pleasure see suffering only as something to be avoided as long as possible. As Banowsky points out, Playboyism "represents a desperate effort to avoid the pain of being a whole person in our kind of world."[3] Hedonists have no word of comfort once suffering arrives. They can detect no possible purpose for it—can see no good that can come from it. Hedonists have no ultimate remedy for any of life's basic ills. "Death is the sovereign remedy for all our misfortunes," wrote Ernest Hemingway in *Death in the Afternoon*. The hedonist seeks by every diversion to escape suffering as long as possible and then await the cure by death. Hemingway's suicide was his way of concluding a life lived on the assumption that good is what you enjoy doing. This makes of life a frantic attempt at a continual holiday.

Addiction—Our drug culture is producing an ever increasing number of people who propose to escape the presence of pain and anguish by means of alcohol and drugs. Getting "high" and taking "trips" may offer temporary relief from the problems of life, but eventually reality must be faced. The longer this is prolonged, the larger the final problem becomes. Anything that solves a man's problems by making him less than himself is a faulty cure. Suffering and pain require the full strength and faculty of any person. Addiction is but a temporary repast that may become the greatest possible source of suffering.

STOICISM

In direct contrast to escapism stands Stoicism. Founded by Zeno in 300 B.C., Stoicism was widespread in the New Testament world and traveling Stoic evangelists were common sights. Stoicism, while stressing moral reformation, is basically pantheisitc. The secret to happiness is to be found by getting in step with nature.

With regard to suffering, Stoicism is apathetic. Without knowing it, many people follow the basic philosophy of Stoicism. Suffering is to be faced with a spirit of self-sufficiency. Early Stoics used the Greek word *autarkes* which Paul uses in Philippians 4:11: "I have learned to be *self-sufficient* under all circumstances" (my translation). The difference between Paul and the Stoics is found in his concluding statement: "I can do all things through Christ which strengtheneth me" (Phil. 4:13). Paul's inner strength comes from Christ. The Stoic generates his own strength, and does it in a very grim way. The Stoic answer to suffering is to so steel oneself that all sensitive and tender emotions are ravished, thus destroying all emotional ties of love and desire that allow one to be hurt by grief and suffering. The Stoic determines to live so that no person or thing is essential to his existence. He strives to arrive at the point where he does not care what happens to anyone, including himself.

Epictetus, an early Stoic, suggested that such a state could be reached by the process of purposely breaking household utensils, and saying, "I don't care." By progressively destroying ever more valuable possessions with the affirmation, "I don't care," the Stoic can come to see a favorite pet die, and not care. At last, he can watch his dearest loved one die, and not care.

The Stoic assumes that everything is ordered by some divine will and must be accepted without struggle. The answer to suffering is to abolish all emotions and desires by steeling the will. T. R. Glover said, "The Stoics made of the heart a desert, and called it peace."

Modern Stoics are known for apathy and are often heard to remark, "We have to grin and bear it," or "That's how the cookie crumbles."[4] Kingsley voices the Stoic outlook poetically:

> For men must work, and women must weep,
> And the sooner it's over, the sooner to sleep;
> And good-bye to the bar and its moaning.[5]

Epictetus suggests that if life becomes too severe, there is a way of escape via suicide. Just as children say, "I won't play any longer," so one can legitimately choose to drop out of the game of life. Epictetus warns, "But if you stay, stop lamenting" (I. xxiv. 20).

In other words, "Pick up your marbles and go home." This alternative to facing everything by sheer personal will is of course another form of escapism, but since it is only an alternative, I have not chosen to place Stoicism with the other escapist answers.

In contrast to the Stoic justification of suicide stands the Christian view expressed by Paul. While in prison, Paul was uncertain as to whether he preferred to live or die, but recognized the decision was not his, but God's. Either way has its good points: "For me to live is Christ, and to die is gain" (Phil. 1:21). To live is to magnify Christ; to die is to be present with Christ.

SCIENTISM

Scientism is another very modern perspective on suffering. It is not to be confused with science, but is rather the worship of science and technology. Such a view believes that, given time, man's know-how will solve every problem. God is no longer a necessary hypothesis.

Ernest Renan, in his *L'avenir de la science* ("The Future of Science"), proclaimed science as a new religion, and himself as priest. He avowed: "Science alone can ameliorate the unhappy situation of man here below."[6]

Bergson points out the failure of the so-called advances of technology: "Humanity groans, half-crushed under the burden of the progress it has made."[7]

Scientism pats the sufferer on the back and says, "Someday we will have a cure," and leaves the inner anguish of conscience, soul, and spirit to endure the pain alone.

This brief survey of some non-Christian perspectives on suffering is at the same time a recognition that each of these perspectives is a religion. Each serves as the center of life for certain people. In his Lowell Lectures, Whitehead warns that religion is not necessarily good, but may indeed be very evil. He states: "In considering religion, we should not be obsessed by the idea of its necessary goodness."[8] It is the character of one's religion that is important.

Whitehead makes it clear that genuine religion (Christianity) is indeed vital to living with suffering: "The fact of the religious vision . . . is our ground for optimism. Apart from it, human life is a flash of occasional enjoyments lighting up a mass of pain and misery."[9]

One reason that no real answers come from the non-Christian perspectives is that only Christianity understands the full dimension of man's basic depravity, and the ultimate reality of good and evil. Only the Christian sees any possible meaning in suffering because only the Christian experiences the presence of a God who cares and purposes. Let us turn now to examine the Christian perspective on suffering. Having examined the poverty of other approaches, perhaps we can now appreciate the Christian outlook, even though it has no simple, clear-cut answers to every problem.

NOTES

1. Leighton Ford, *The Christian Persuader* (New York: Harper & Row, Publishers, 1966), p. 103.
2. David O. Woodyard, *Living Without God—Before God* (Philadelphia: The Westminster Press, 1968), pp. 74-75.
3. William S. Banowsky, *It's a Playboy World* (Old Tappan, NJ: Fleming H. Revell Co., 1969), p. 32.
4. George Buttrick, *God, Pain, and Evil* (New York: Abingdon Press, 1966), p. 140.
5. Charles Kingsley, "The Three Fishers," stanza 3.
6. Paul Tournier, *The Whole Person in a Broken World* (New York: Harper & Row, Publishers, 1947), p. 91.
7. Ibid., p. 123.
8. A. N. Whitehead, *Religion in the Making* (New York: The Macmillan Company, 1927), p. 18.
9. A. N. Whitehead, *Science and the Modern World* (New York: Cambridge University Press), p. 238.

2

The Christian Perspective

> "And we know that to them that love God, all things work together for good, even to them that are called according to his purpose" (Rom. 8:28).

While the Christian perspective offers the only meaningful approach to suffering, we must admit that suffering poses a bigger problem for the Christian than for anyone else because the Christian must attempt to relate God to the dimension of human suffering.

Also, we must beware of oversimplification. To affirm with Paul that "God is able to bring good out of any circumstance in the lives of those who love him" (Rom. 8:28, translation mine) is not to set up a stand for the dispensing of easy answers.

The presupposition of men like Leibniz that this is the best of all possible worlds can be made to mean that everything that happens is good. Neither the words of the Bible nor the experiences of life affirm this. Much that happens is bad. Voltaire over-reacted (no doubt purposefully) to men like Leibniz in his novel, *Candide* ("Optimism"). Voltaire uses humorous satire to ridicule the simple answers of Candide's tutor, Dr. Pangloss, who affirmed that every event was for the best. Early in the novel Candide learns that the woman he adores, Lady Cunegonde, has been ravished by marauding soldiers, disemboweled, and cut into small pieces. The man defending her had his head bashed in. The house had been completely demolished and all the livestock taken.

Similar experiences befall Candide and the other characters throughout the novel, yet Pangloss affirms that every event is for the best. The world expects some answers to life's dilemmas, but is not impressed with naive replies that do not jibe with life's experiences. From the Christian fold in recent years have come various approaches centered around the concept of positive thinking as exemplified by Norman Vincent Peale.

Peale's answers to life's pains are too simple. Peale tends to have an easy formula designed to bring victory over every problem. By certain attitudes, and by the repetition of certain Scripture passages, man is able to venture forth each day and succeed. Peale stands dangerously close to Christian Science in its denial of evil. Peale uses a metaphor from golf and claims that "the rough is only mental."[1] Again, this "mind over matter" approach is closely akin to the Christian Science concept that mind is all. No doubt Peale's emphasis upon the power of positive thinking has helped many. What a man thinks is terribly important. But there are painful experiences in life which do not respond to positive thinking. We must approach the world's sickbed with great reverence and humility. We have no easy cure-all.

THE UNIVERSE

Perhaps the place to begin our formulation of the Christian view of suffering is the universe itself. What kind of world order do we have? Three possibilities present themselves. The universe may be governed by blind chance; by mechanical, natural laws; or by divine providence. Only the latter is an option for the Christian for it alone allows the possibility of purpose.

While God is the author of natural law, He is not its prisoner. He stands above it and uses it as He pleases. Science has increasingly become aware that natural law is not as rigid as it once supposed. There are many unexplained variations that occur.

C. S. Lewis reminds the naturalist that he has mistaken a part of the system (nature) for the whole (which is nature plus the supernatural). The natural laws resemble a computer. The only thing necessary to change the outcome is the feeding of new events into the pattern. Thus God's activity above nature permits such additions that in turn bring about new results. Hence a "miracle" takes place. Nature, when impregnated by divine action, gives birth quite naturally to miracles.[2]

In fact, God deals in the miraculous. The main plot is not to be found in atoms, politics, or economics. C. S. Lewis illustrates the way God's real plot is often missed by telling of a playwright who wrote about a hero having a pathological horror of trees with a mania for cutting them down. The plot centered around the conflict of the hero with the trees. As a side feature, the playwright added a love story and a few other trappings. Yet when he sent the play to another writer for evaluation, the reply was: "Not bad, but I'd cut out those bits of padding about the trees."[3] The main plot had been missed.

MAN'S FREEDOM

A world where the miraculous is possible is complicated by the freedom divinely bestowed upon man. If man is to be a real person instead of a robot he must be free to make choices. God has allowed this freedom. Man holds in his hands the possibility of good and evil. Frankl reminds us that "man is that being who has invented the gas chambers of Auschwitz; however, he is also that being who has entered those gas chambers upright, with the Lord's Prayer or the Shema Yisrael on his lips."[4]

Man develops atomic power, and uses it for bombs. His capacity for love is offset by his power to hate. He can give his life in selfless service or he can become a miserly scrooge. Yet it must be so, for unless man has the power to choose evil, his choice of good will be meaningless. Yet this power to choose is also the power to inflict harm on others, as well as on self.

GOD'S WILL

Now we begin to see the complexity of the problem

of suffering. If we could deal only with a world open to miracles and a loving, all-powerful God, we could have a world void of all pain. But standing between such a world and such a God is the freedom of man, and of depraved man at that. Man's freedom forbids our attributing every event to the will of God.

I am convinced that very few things that happen are the will of God. I find very few people doing the will of God. Since God is all powerful, we are forced to confess that nothing can occur unless God permits it.

I performed the funeral of a young man who was slain by an estranged husband. The husband had found the two together and murder resulted. Nothing about the tragedy could be construed as God's will. Yet the fact that God did not intervene means that in a sense He permitted it to happen. Therefore we cannot adequately deal with the will of God without breaking the subject up into at least two parts: the permissive will of God and the purposeful will of God.

God's permissive will —God operates within the tension of carrying out His divine purposes and respecting man's freedom of choice. The only way God could have prevented the murder mentioned above would have been to overrule the free choice of either the secret lovers, or the irate husband.

Added to man's freedom is the element of evil propagated by Satan. It is the satanic presence that heightens the explosive danger of human freedom. God permits this satanic power to operate, thus making man's choice a real one. Jesus Himself, confronted by the satanic, said: "My kingdom is not of this world" (John 18:36). Our world is one where God can be slapped (John 18:22), insulted, and crucified.

The question, "Where was God when my son was killed?" coming from the lips of a grief-stricken parent, was well answered by the minister: "Just where He was when His own Son was killed."5

God's very character forbids His playing favorites, even with His own Son. The young Christian wife who suffered and died of leukemia was permitted to do so. Weatherhead rightly reminds us that if God allowed only the ungodly to succumb to disease, everyone would look upon religion as an insurance against suffering and "rush to pay the premium with a spurious piety."[6]

God is placed in the position of having to always see the whole picture, the total human family. He must think not only in temporal terms but also must consider eternal implications. Dr. Crichton-Miller illustrates this in terms of a mother who pleads with the stationmaster to hold a train for an additional fifteen minutes in order for her husband to arrive. Their son was dying and the only chance to see him alive was to catch that train. The stationmaster explained he could not possibly delay the departure since to do so might cause even more serious problems to other people trying to make connections.[7] God is faced with running a universe and we cannot expect Him to stop the world for us.

God's purposeful will —What then does God intend for us? What is His will? The Bible reminds us that God is busy bringing "good out of every circumstance in the lives of those that love him" (Rom. 8:28). The primary question that must be answered is: What is the *summum bonum,* the supreme good? Man has his ready answers to that question, but it is God's answer that we must have.

Weatherhead states that God wills health for every person.[8] To be sure, God has our welfare at heart, and suffering has no virtue within itself. However, health and happiness are not the supreme good. Above all else, God wants us to be Christlike. The good which He seeks to bring out of every circumstance is that each of us might be "conformed to the image of his Son" (Rom. 8:29). This is the *good* with which God is first of all concerned. He wants us to think like Christ, love like Christ, care like Christ, obey like Christ, and sacrifice like Christ. Whatever attempts to defeat this divine purpose will have to deal with God. The interference of satanic forces, the careless choices of other men, and our own human failures may force God to improvise, to set up ways other than the ideal to mold us into Christlikeness, but He will not be defeated!

As we recognize God's supreme purpose (that of making us Christlike), we get a new glimpse of the humility with which we must pray, for often "we know not what we should pray for as we ought" (Rom. 8:26). The escape which we seek might hinder our spiritual progress. The pain which we desire to avoid might well make of us spoiled and pampered snobs. While it is just and proper for us to ask God for healing, we must remember that should He fail to intervene it is not a sign that our faith is faulty.

The travesty committed by most faith healers is the impression they leave that real faith produces real miracles. No miracle—no faith. Nothing could be further from the truth. One of the most faithful men of all times, the apostle Paul, had a physical malady for which he asked divine healing on three distinct and separate occasions (II Cor. 12:7-10). Yet he was not healed.

Many of the so-called successes of faith healers are in the psychosomatic realm. The emotionalism of the healing service banishes the physical symptom and they pronounce themselves healed. The danger involved is that the psychological condition which set up the physical symptom, unless healed also, will produce another symptom, probably even more severe. The new disorder may well be located in the mind bringing on mental suffering, perhaps even nervous breakdowns.[9]

Canon Grensted illustrates this danger in a story about a doctor who cured a patient of the obsession that he was a dog. There was, however, one problem. The patient then decided he was a water-rat.[10]

This is not to say that God does not perform healing miracles. He does. But He does not dispense them on a wholesale basis. The Bible seems to indicate that miracles are reserved for the carrying out of God's redemptive purposes. We live in a world where the miraculous is possible. We worship a God who loves, and is all powerful. Rather than destroy man's freedom God permits things to happen—things with which He is not pleased. Yet He will not be defeated, nor will He allow His children to be ultimately defeated. He purposes to make us Christlike. This is the stance with which we face evil and suffering. Everything does not turn out for the best. For the unbeliever, nothing turns out for the best. By rejecting Christ he has rejected all possibility of meaning and purpose. For the believer, the child of God, everything that happens is not good, but if turned over to God, can have something good salvaged from it. As a child, we come to the heavenly Father with our griefs and pains, assured that He cares, and that He will not allow anything to defeat His ultimate purpose for our lives. Just how God is able to use our suffering will be discussed in detail in Part Three.

Notes

1. Merrill Proudfoot, *Suffering: A Christian Understanding* (Philadelphia: The Westminster Press, 1964), pp. 67-68.
2. C. S. Lewis, *Miracles* (London: Collins Clear-type Press, 1947), pp. 64ff.
3. Ibid., p. 103.
4. Viktor Frankl, *Man's Search for Meaning* (New York: Washington Square Press, Inc., 1963), pp. 213-14.
5. George Buttrick, *God, Pain, and Evil* (Nashville: Abingdon Press, 1966), pp. 166-67.
6. Leslie D. Weatherhead, *Salute to a Sufferer* (New York: Abingdon Press, 1962), pp. 51-52.
7. Ibid., pp. 36-37.
8. Ibid., p. 13.
9. Ibid., pp. 83-84.
10. Ibid., quoting L. W. Grensted, *Psychology and God* (London: Longmans, Green & Co., Ltd., 1930), p. 117.

Part Two

CAUSES OF SUFFERING

3

Impersonal Causes for Suffering

Rather than curse God for all suffering, as Job's wife suggested, we do well to consider other forces from whence come pain and grief. We have already observed that man's power to choose is also the power to inflict harm. Granted that man brings much suffering on himself, and that God is personally involved in some suffering (this will be discussed in chapter 4), we need to be aware of other factors and forces that figure in the human dilemma.

THE FALLEN WORLD OF NATURE

The tragedy of the human story began in the Garden of Eden. Since man's first act of rebellion, he has been separated from an environment totally friendly to him. This is the significance of man's being driven from Eden.

Man's fall, his act of rebellion, was not experienced in solitary confinement. His whole environment was affected. There is a sense in which the natural world fell along with man. To be sure, the world of nature did not sin, for natural law is impersonal. Yet man's fall required a divine rearrangement of nature. Man had been forewarned that rebellion would bring the curse of death (Gen. 2:17). Whereas man's act of rebellion was an attempt to play god over the world of creation, now he must die at the hands of that world of nature. The world must become a dangerous place to live—so dangerous that no man can escape death!

A Scriptural framework for such an outlook comes from the apostle Paul: "For nature did not of its own accord give up to failure; it was for the sake of Him who let it thus be given up, in the hope that even nature itself might be finally set free from its bondage to decay, so as to share the glorious freedom of God's children" (Rom. 8:20-21, Williams Translation).

Nature is personified in order to be pictured as waiting on tiptoe to get a glimpse of what God has planned for His children in eternity (Rom. 8:19) when even the natural world will be changed (Rev. 21:1).

God's rearrangement of nature to carry out the sentence of death causes Paul to observe: "Yes, we know that all nature has gone on groaning in agony together till the present moment" (Rom. 8:22, Williams Translation). Therefore neither man nor nature has been the same since Eden's rebellion. Understanding something of the turmoil in which man lives, the Christian joins in nature's anxious travail, awaiting the birth of God's eternity: "We ourselves who enjoy the Spirit as a foretaste of the future, even we ourselves, keep up our inner groanings while we wait to enter upon our adoption as God's sons at the redemption of our bodies" (Rom. 8:23, Williams Translation).

The law of the jungle.—Now an examination of the natural world will prove helpful. To be sure, there are many moot questions. Was man the only creation who could have lived forever? The Bible does not answer this question. However, it would seem that the lower species of life, plant and animal, were created to keep a balance within nature. This would require that death be a part of that world. We must keep in mind that death in animals, and so forth, is different from death in man. Only man knows he must die and is capable of having concern with time and the dimension of past and future.

The balance of nature is an amazing phenomenon which we have only begun to understand. F. A. Filby explains that while sharks may eat cod, and cod may live on herring, the herring requires a mixed diet of the smaller plankton. One herring may consume 6,000 of these tiny creatures at one meal. They in turn feed on algae, requiring 100,000 tiny plants—diatoms—for a meal. These diatoms must also be fed by the phosphates, silicates, and calcium washed from the continental rocks and delivered by the rivers.[1]

Each day we discover new tasks performed by the species of lower life. Birds, for instance, serve as God's gardeners by carrying seeds as well as serving as nature's scavengers. Michelet says, "Birds can live without men, but man cannot live without birds." Small insects would ruin the world in less than ten years were they not controlled by birds. Similar illustrations are available on every level of the natural world.[2]

Keeping a proper balance of nature, making human life possible, requires the cycle of death. The pain of such death is not to be equated with human pain. On the biologist's scale of the ability of different species to suffer pain, the earthworm and the oyster are very low. The more developed species show an increase in the capacity to experience pain. But no animal suffering is as intense, nor as capable of anxiety and anguish, as is man's.

The tragedy of Eden is that man chose to go it alone, to lower himself to the animal level and thus to participate in the law of the jungle, a law for which he was not intended.

Disease —Modern science, using God-given wisdom, is engaged in a constant struggle against disease. But why germs in the first place? Leslie Weatherhead has written effectively in this area.[3] In much the same way that our forefathers shot wolves, we battle germs that, like a wolf pack, would descend upon us. But why such microscopic wolf-packs?

Some scientific findings indicate disease to be much older than man. The fossilized bones of a prehistoric reptile that lived 130 million years ago indicate the animal suffered from osteomyelitis. The remains of one dinosaur indicate bone tumor.[4]

As we contemplate the origin of germs, we need to remember that not all are harmful. In fact, much bacteria found in the human body are friendly and health-producing. They feed on bodily secretions. Dr. J. G. Adami, after much research, writes that these friendly and unfriendly (virulent and nonvirulent) microbes often live side by side, differing little except that one is harmful and the other helpful. Dr. Adami's conclusion is that the disease-producing microbes probably originated from the healthful ones at some period of development. He says, "According to the environment so do bacteria assume special qualities."[5]

There are many theories about how friendly bacteria become unfriendly. One interesting one, in light of Dr. Adami's theory, is illustrated in a case described by Eric Pritchard in *Infant Education*. A baby died while being breast-fed by his mother. The nursing mother was forced to watch a struggle between her husband and a man whom she hated for having sought to seduce her. The mother's hate was of such intensity that the milk in her breast was turned to poison. Her baby died almost instantly.[6] If an intense emotion like hate can change the chemical components of the breast glands, then it seems quite possible that such emotions could change the secretion of mucous by the mucous glands—a mucous on which many friendly bacteria live. Perhaps such a change could make friendly bacteria malignant.

Dr. Adami sees the simplest explanation of diphtheria as being due to a previously harmless bacillus, growing in the throat and upper respiratory passages, coming to acquire virulent properties.

If such be the case, who knows what diseases are the result of the sins of rebellion, hate, and envy, on the part of Adam, and of ourselves. The existence of disease germs before the creation of man does not mean that man was meant to be sick. Disease could have been a part of the animal world without invading the human story. Even yet the body has an amazing immunity to harmful germs. When man chose to come under the law of death, by virtue of his sin he may well have surrendered his total immunity to disease, allowing nature to carry out the process of death. How much we help create diseases, and hasten our own death by sinful emotions of hate and bitterness, we are only beginning to discover.

Natural calamities —The divine rearrangement of nature from that of a protective environment to that of a dangerous one, allowing for human death as punishment of sin, permits nature to go on the rampage. Part of its "groaning" (Rom. 8:22) includes the area of natural catastrophe, floods, earthquakes, and hurricanes.

However, a cautious approach is necessary when determining an event of nature to be a calamity. Sometimes the rain that saves the farmer's crops floods the reservoir, washing out the dam and drowning those who live down the valley. The needs of the various segments of the world's family are often in conflict. Who can see the whole picture?

Buttrick points out that the Niagara River is a thing of joy for the people having summer homes at Grand Isle. Yet the same river has been the source of many tragedies at the Falls. Strangely enough, however, more people are attracted to the awesome and tragic Falls than to Grand Isle. The unleashed energy of the Falls, that brings death, is also the source of electricity to light dark homes.[7]

It seems quite possible that the rampages of nature serve to keep man from a false sense of well-being and security. Joel lived through a devastating locust plague and was led to view it as a divine means to remind the Israelites of a frightful day yet to come—the Day of Judgment (Joel 2).

We who are so prone to settle for this world need to be reminded that this world is unsettled. In fact, every aspect of the fallen natural world not only contributes to man's death, but also points man toward divine deliverance. Only God can save us from such a world.

Satan has a toehold on our present existence—a toehold granted by man's rebellion against God. He seems not to be without power. God permitted Satan the use of natural calamity and disease to prove the reality of

Job's faith (a subject about which more will be said later).

As powerful as Satan is, and as dangerous as the natural world is, we do not despair. As Christians we choose not to limit our existence to the earthly. Life still has meaning and value because we have chosen to include the spiritual dimension with our physical existence, to add the supernatural to the natural. The natural world does not, therefore, determine our future. We join with Habakkuk in asserting: "Although the fig tree shall not blossom, neither shall fruit be in the vines; the labour of the olive shall fail, and the fields shall yield no meat; the flock shall be cut off from the fold, and there shall be no herd in the stalls: yet I will rejoice in the Lord, I will joy in the God of my salvation" (Hab. 3:17-18).

THE MORAL UNIVERSE

Conscience —Immanuel Kant reminded the world that man has a sense of moral oughtness.[8] One of the classic arguments for the existence of God is that man has a conscience, divinely given and guided. Man has moral experiences and feels an obligation to do right.

Cause and effect —W. R. Sorley further reminds us that the world has a way of sustaining moral persons.[9] Over the long haul, the good life experiences a reward of its own, while the evil life at last suffers deterioration in one way or another. William Hocking observes that a person who loves his enemy, as divinely ordered, will be profited in the long run, far more than any gain he could have hoped for by onslaught.[10]

Just as natural law is observable in nature, so moral law is revealed by a study of man's choices, and the resultant good or evil that comes. There is a moral system of cause and effect that operates, however slowly. This is not to say that every sin is punished in this life by a moral universe, for there is a final reckoning that lies ahead—a Day of Judgment. Yet immoral living does bring about its own destruction because God has so constituted our world. Breathing under water results in death. So sin brings disaster and suffering.

In a world where mental hospitals are filled, O. Hobart Mowrer, Research Professor of Psychology at the University of Illinois, states his studies indicate anxiety to be the result of guilt—not guilt feelings—but genuine guilt derived from having committed acts which later are regretted.[11] Few areas of suffering exceed the anguish of mental illness, to say nothing of the many physical ailments so induced.

Moral absolutes —Any quarrel is predicated on the assumption that someone is right and someone is wrong. C. S. Lewis observes that some kind of law regarding decent behavior is found in every civilization, and that there is a basic similarity to be discovered in these laws. No country admires a coward. No man feels proud for having betrayed those who befriended him. Cultures may differ as to whether a man should have a plurality of wives, but cultures have always said that a man should not have any and every woman he sees. To prefer Christian morality to Nazi morality is meaningless unless there is a basic, built-in standard by which to make such a comparison.[12]

The Ten Commandments are the basis of the moral law of the universe. They are the key to an understanding of life. Rather than being objective commands, they reveal the secret to a full life. They set forth the way of life that can be blessed. To transgress them is to fly in the face of a morally constituted universe which includes the make-up of the human soul.

Romans portrays the devastation wrought by moral trangression (Rom. 1:21-32). Every kind of sin and deviation is depicted with the resultant statement: "God gave them up." He left them to themselves and the havoc, inner and outer, which comes upon immorality in a morally constituted universe containing morally constituted beings. Men who ignore God's moral laws bring suffering upon themselves and upon their loved ones.

Human experience —There is no paucity of human

examples with regard to self-destruction by living outside the moral law. The Bible relates the story of Haman, a man destroyed by his own hate. Living on bitterness and vengeance, he poisoned himself. Any time a man decides to plot the destiny of others, to conceive their ruin, he steps outside the prescribed realm of his morality, and suffers the delusion of a God-complex. Haman's hatred for Mordecai leads him to devise a sinister plot designed to bring about Mordecai's execution. At the last moment, everything boomerangs. Haman is hanged on his own scaffold! The king has seen through him. What we must understand is that even had the plot succeeded, Haman would have lost. There can be no inner happiness in a heart where hate dwells. We are so constituted.

Samson stands as the example of a man ruined by lust. He tried to mix religion with his Playboyism and ended life in utter defeat. The lure of forbidden women led to the breaking of his religious vows. Disaster was sure to come. All that remained uncertain were the details.

Gibbon's classic work on the fall of the Roman Empire is but another historical proof of the operation of a moral law. Many of the reasons Gibbon cites for the fall of Rome are direct violations of the Ten Commandments. Every civilization that becomes morally corrupt, fails. There have been no exceptions.

Buttrick compares the tapping out of historical events to the code of the telegraph. The message may be slow in coming, but there is a message. Men who are willing to read these events recognize in them a private code with a personal message.[13] *Immorality always produces suffering in a moral universe.*

NOTES

1. F. A. Filby, *Creation Revealed* (Westwood, NJ: Fleming H. Revell Company, 1963), p. 98.
2. Ibid., p. 105-06.
3. Leslie D. Weatherhead, *Salute to a Sufferer* (New York: Abingdon Press, 1962), pp. 48-72.
4. G. G. Dawson, *Healing, Pagan and Christian* (London: S.P.C.K., 1935), pp. 1-3.
5. J. G. Adami, *Medical Contributions to the Study of Evolution* (London: Duckworth, 1918), pp. 23-24, quoted by Weatherhead, *Salute*.
6. Quoted by Weatherford, *Salute*, p. 68-69.
7. Buttrick, *God, Pain, and Evil* (Nashville: Abingdon Press, 1966), pp. 54-55.
8. Cf. Immanuel Kant, *Critique of Practical Reason.*
9. Cf. W. R. Sorley, *Moral Values and the Idea of God.*
10. Cf. William Hocking, *Human Nature in Its Remaking.*
11. O. Hobart Mowrer, *The Crisis in Psychiatry and Religion* (New York: D. Van Nostrand Company, Inc., 1961), pp. 26ff.
12. C. S. Lewis, *The Case for Christianity* (New York: The Macmillan Company, 1965), pp. 3-12.
13. Buttrick, *God, Pain, and Evil*, pp. 52-53.

4

Divine Chastisement

> "And ye have forgotten the exhortation which speaketh unto you as unto children, My son, despise not thou the chastening of the Lord, nor faint when thou art rebuked of him: For whom the Lord loveth he chasteneth, and scourgeth every son whom he receiveth" (Heb. 12:5-6).

"Is this God's way of punishing me for my sins?" The question came from a distraught mother who had just learned that her son was suffering from an incurable disease. The possibility that one's suffering is a direct result of God's personal punishment haunts many people as they lie in hospital beds or stand in funeral parlors.

Most of us would feel relieved if we could dismiss the concept of personal wrath on the part of God. Theologians like C. H. Dodd see God's wrath as merely a Biblical expression to describe the retribution meted out by a moral universe that operates impersonally according to divine laws.[1] However, such a view discounts ample Biblical evidence to the contrary. The idea of a holy God reacting in a personal way to the sins of men is everywhere portrayed in Holy Writ.

However, a word of caution is needed. We can never determine whether someone else's suffering is a result of God's personal administration of punishment. The mother's question: "Is this God's way of punishing me for my sins?" is something no one else can answer for her. If it is punishment, God will reveal it to her. Now another word of caution. Guilt complexes being what they are, together with the fact that all of us have sinned, combine to make it difficult for us to know for certain. That mother may assume God has impressed her with the knowledge that her anguish is divine chastisement when in reality her son is but the victim of a fallen world ravished by disease, and she the victim of a guilty conscience. A good rule to follow is to assume that all suffering is the result of a fallen world of nature or a morally constituted universe unless you are unusually and clearly impressed that God is personally punishing you.

The concept of a God who inflicts punishment does injustice to Him unless we recognize that His wrath is not whimsical or spasmodic. He is not given to fits of temper. His wrath is as dependable and constant as His love. In fact, the two are but different sides of the same coin—of His righteousness (His just and impartial way of doing things). Further, we must differentiate between God's punishment of believers and unbelievers.

CHASTISEMENT OF BELIEVERS

Commitment to Jesus Christ admits us into God's family. We become a child of God. The all-powerful creator of the universe becomes our heavenly Father. His discipline is administered in parental love. Like children, we have trouble believing the old cliche: "This is going to hurt me more than you." Discipline is a necessary part of the parental role, but it never is appreciated by the child during the momentary administration of it: "Now no chastening for the present seemeth to be joyous, but grievous" (Heb. 12:11). As God's children, regardless of our age, we still must live under His discipline. Unless we are careful, we will still pout, feel sorry for ourselves, or become discouraged.

The writer of Hebrews addresses Jewish Christians who are living under severe persecution. The life of faith is bringing problems instead of peace, distress instead of deliverance. To the discouraged he writes: "Lift up the hands which hang down, and the feeble knees" (Heb. 12:12). He reminds them of the importance that discipline plays in the Christian experience: "Despise not thou the chastening of the Lord, nor faint when thou art rebuked of him" (Heb. 12:5). The word translated "despise" means "to make light of," and the word "chastening" carries the idea of parental training that sometimes involves chastisement. This is not an easy world in which to stand for righteousness. Our age is not congenial toward Christian values and morality.

C. S. Lewis reminds us that suffering is God's megaphone with which He penetrates our deafness.[2] Sometimes this is the only way God can get our attention. Now the dangerous thing about discipline is that, while it is designed to draw us nearer the Lord, it may also drive us away unless we understand why God permits it, or administers it, as the case may be. There are times when God stands by and allows a sinful world to mistreat us, as a part of our discipline. Other times God dips into our human story to divinely punish us. There are some definite reasons that we should never pout when chastening comes.

Chastening is the sign of a loving Father —Why does God allow His children to suffer, to be mistreated? Because He loves us: "For whom the Lord loveth he chasteneth, and scourgeth every son whom he receiveth" (Heb. 12:6). The wise parent must often stand by and allow his child to be bullied and misused, for if the parent steps in to fight the battle, his child will never learn to stand on his own two feet. Other times a father is forced to stand helplessly and watch his child make wrong choices that bring severe penalties. The Prodigal Son is the story of such a father. There was no doubt that the wayward son was headed for heartbreak. Yet because the father loved, he allowed the son to leave home, trusting that the resultant chastening would bring him back someday. There are other times when a parent must actively administer correction, especially if he sets his children forth as examples of what children ought to be. Since the heavenly Father has decreed that His children are to be the light of the world, He must be concerned about their behavior.

Chastening, when properly understood, brings assurance of sonship: "If ye endure chastening, God dealeth with you as sons; for what son is he whom the father chasteneth not?" (Heb. 12:7). Never be guilty of complaining because the ungodly seem to get off scot-free while you are chastened on every hand. The ungodly are destined for eternal punishment. Only the child of God is promised punishment in this life. The real cause for worry would be for you to remain unchastened in your earthly sojourn. Jerome's words are very true: "The greatest anger of all is when God is no longer angry with us when we sin."[3] The fact that God cares enough to correct us is proof of His love.

Chastening is part of training toward Christlikeness —
To confess Christ as Lord is to begin a journey toward being remade in His likeness. "Chastening" is the ordinary Greek word for education.[4] In Acts 7:22 the same word is translated "learned": "And Moses was learned in all the wisdom of the Egyptians." However the word usually carries the idea of moral training brought about by discipline, which is certainly how the writer of Hebrews uses it. Interestingly enough, the Revised Version renders Hebrews 12:7: "It is for chastening that ye endure." This makes chastening (moral instruction) the purpose for which the Christian should be willing to endure all things.

Jonah is an example of a man God had to "educate." Ordered to go to Nineveh, the capital city of the hated Assyrians, and preach repentance, Jonah rebelled and took the first ship going in the opposite direction. Jonah hated the people of Nineveh for they were barbaric and cruel. They were his nation's enemy. He preferred their doom rather than their salvation. Only as God's hand lay heavily on him and death seemed certain did Jonah learn the necessity of obedience.

Michelet tells how the roaming cattle in hot countries are driven out of the swampy lowlands into the higher hill country by the furious insects. In reality, the painful insects save the cattle from the diseases so prevalent among livestock in the feverish lowlands. The parallel is easily evident when applied to the part discipline and hardship play in Christian growth. Sometimes our sorrows drive us from the dangerous swamp lands of an easy life into the pure alpine air of God's higher purposes.[5]

Buttrick reminds us that if it were not for pain, we would never have known God. Only pain is able to break our grip on this world and divert our gaze from temporary pursuits.[6] Pain is the divine scalpel with which God performs spiritual surgery, thereby making us into the image of Christ. The apostle Paul describes his physical suffering in terms of a thorn that causes constant pain as it jostles and irritates and corrupts. Yet he affirms that God's purpose in allowing such suffering is to remind him of his own weakness, thus magnifying God's strength and grace, which is sufficient. Such experiences keep us mindful of our mission, and our source of deliverance. Knowing this, Paul explains his attitude toward pain: "Therefore I take pleasure in infirmities, in reproaches, in necessities, in persecutions, in distresses for Christ's sake: for when I am weak, then am I strong" (II Cor. 12:10).

When we are tempted to ask why God permits us to suffer, or why He chastens us, we must remember that to shield us from pain would be to stunt our growth toward Christlikeness. Our supreme goal is to become like Christ, of whom it is said: "Though he were a Son, yet learned he obedience by the things which he suffered" (Heb. 5:8).

Huxley completely misunderstands the place of pain in his novel, *Brave New World*. He pictures the future as a time when God and Christianity are but forgotten superstitions amidst an enlightened scientific world. Any time pain, or any distasteful event, occurs the people merely take a drug called *soma* which makes any situation pleasant.

Instead of numbing ourselves from hardships, we

would do better to invite them as we would much-needed surgery. The psalmist observes: "Weeping may endure for a night, but joy cometh in the morning" (Ps. 30:5). H. Wheeler Robinson calls our attention to the literal Hebrew meaning that pictures weeping as a guest who comes to stay overnight.[7] He may have a horrible, fearsome appearance, but hospitality demands he be invited inside. Beyond the brief night of this earthly life, we will awaken to find that the dangerous visitor was sent to help us, and that will call forth rapturous joy.

A Stoicism that seeks to steel itself against pain to develop complete apathy shuts out one of the greatest sources of direction to be found in the human situation. We are not merely to endure suffering, we are to learn from it and be remade by it. We do not flee from pain, but rather reach out in the midst of it to find the grace of God's healing presence.

The pitiful plight of man in the twentieth century is that he has all he wants, and his "all" leaves God out. Augustine observes: "God wants to give us something but cannot, because our hands are full—there's nowhere for Him to put it."[8] Therefore God's chastening must come to take away our false gods with which we are so enraptured.

Instead of pouting, we must realize the full goal toward which God is leading. God really does do it for our own good: "That we might be partakers of his holiness" (Heb. 12:10). The basic idea of holiness is to be set apart, to be different. God wants us to be different from unredeemed men, to be set apart for His service, so He chastens us. He loves us enough to care about us, to correct us, to let us become wiser through suffering. Hardship is the divine gymnasium wherein we build our spiritual muscles by endless workouts: "Now no chastening for the present seemeth to be joyous, but grievous: nevertheless afterward it yieldeth the peaceable fruit of righteousness unto them which are exercised thereby" (Heb. 12:11).

CHASTISEMENT OF UNBELIEVERS

God's chastisement of unbelievers seems to fall into a different category. He cannot deal with them as a parent for they have rejected His offered Fatherhood. He cannot direct them toward Christlikeness for they have rejected Christ. Indeed there are times when it seems God pretty well lets the unbeliever go his own way unchecked except for the impersonal power of a fallen world and a moral universe.

The psalmist was quite upset by the fact that the wicked seem to get the best of it: "My steps had well nigh slipped. For I was envious at the foolish, when I saw the prosperity of the wicked" (Ps. 73:2b-3). The psalmist observed that often the wicked enjoy excellent health, long lives, and easy deaths (Ps. 73:4-5). Only as the psalmist considered the final destiny of the wicked was he able to understand God's apparent slackness: "It was too painful for me; until I went into the sanctuary of God; then understood I their end" (Ps. 73:16b-17).

Since God's final settlement comes in eternity, He need be in no hurry to correct the unbelievers. While He may occasionally use chastisement in an effort to awaken unbelievers, He seems to limit most of His direct interventions to those times when His broad purposes are being endangered. The Flood came upon all men when wickedness had gotten out of hand. The Lord afflicted Pharaoh's Egypt with a series of ten plagues when it became apparent that only such action would bring the release of the Israelites from slavery and allow their journey to Canaan. When Pharaoh had second thoughts and sent his army to bring back the Israelites, God drowned the army in the sea.

When God sought to release His people from Babylonian exile, He wrote a message on the banquet wall in the presence of the haughty Belshazzar: "God hath numbered thy kingdom, and finished it. . . . Thou art weighed in the balances, and art found wanting. . . . Thy kingdom is divided and given to the Medes and Persians" (Dan. 5:27-28). Humanly speaking, Cyrus deposed Belshazzar and took his kingdom. The Scriptures tell us God was the director of the drama. God counts no price too big to pay; no empire too powerful to uproot; no potentate too mighty to dethrone; when His purposes are at stake.

To summarize for a moment, God chastises His children in this life in order to keep them on course and make their lives purposeful. He assures them they have no need to fear a final judgment (John 5:24). The believer's judgment comes in this life and is administered by a loving Father. Simon Peter has this in mind when he states: "Judgment must begin at the house of God: and if it first begin at us, what shall be the end of them that obey not the gospel of God?" (I Peter 4:17-18).

Whereas God chastises and purifies His children in this life, He reserves the judgment of the unbelievers until eternity, with occasional exceptions when His purposes are at stake: "The Lord knoweth how to . . . reserve the unjust unto the day of judgment to be punished" (II Peter 2:9). Whereas the Christian's daily judgment issues in his ultimate salvation and transformation, the unbeliever's judgment inaugurates his eternal despair. Do not envy the carefree spirit of the ungodly. He has the only good he will ever have.

NOTES

1. C. H. Dodd, *The Epistle of Paul to the Romans* (London: Fontana Books, 1959), p. 55.
2. C. S. Lewis, *The Problem of Pain* (New York: The Macmillan Company, 1962), p. 93.
3. William Barclay, *The Letter to the Hebrews* (Edinburgh: The Saint Andrew Press, 1955), p. 203.
4. James Hastings (ed.), "The Epistle to the Hebrews" in *The Speaker's Bible* (Grand Rapids: Baker Book House, 1961), p. 300.
5. Ibid., p. 302.
6. George Buttrick, *God, Pain, and Evil* (Nashville: Abingdon Press, 1966), p. 175.
7. Ibid., quoting H. Wheeler Robinson, p. 157.
8. Lewis, *Problem of Pain*, p. 96.

Part Three
THE ROLE OF SUFFERING

5

Suffering As Education

> I walked a mile with Pleasure,
>   She chattered all the way,
> But left me none the wiser,
>   For all she had to say.
>
> I walked a mile with Sorrow,
>   And ne'er a word said she;
> But, oh, the things I learned from her
>   When Sorrow walked with me![1]

Life is a school and suffering is one of the instructors. For this reason Christians are not exempt. The heavenly Father cares too much about us to let us go on in ignorance. He desires our maturity, and maturity does not come easily. Some lessons are never learned apart from suffering.

When I was a boy, I thought my parents were very strict. They reprimanded me for tiny (at least they seemed tiny to me) infractions. They expected me to study hard in school and do my best. I had friends who got away with "murder," whose parents laughed at their pranks and cared less about their studies. Throughout the summer months on the farm I worked in the fields alongside grown men doing as much work as they while some of my friends splashed about in the swimming hole. I operated powerful machinery while my father kept a watchful eye on my every move, constantly correcting me far beyond what was necessary for acceptable performance.

But as I look back on those experiences, I understand that my parents were trying to teach me the importance of doing my best. They were trying to teach me responsibility. I think they cared more about my future than the parents of some of my friends cared about theirs. In much the same fashion, God corrects us and plans for our future. He has many means at His disposal, but His omnipotence enables Him to even use suffering as a means of instruction.

For some reason man learns more from disasters than from blessings. It seems that some things are learned only from disaster. This does not mean we are not capable of learning apart from disaster, but that we are not willing to do so. We are not willing to face the truth until we are forced to.

The child who is warned against touching the hot stove could heed the warning, but seldom does. The teen-ager who is warned against the evils of alcohol could heed the warning, but usually decides to find out for himself. Sometimes he learns his lesson while lying amidst the twisted wreckage of a car, sometimes years later in the grips of alcoholic tremors, and sometimes he never learns.

The teen-age girl who discounts her parents' warning about sexual promiscuity sometimes learns her lesson while waiting for the birth of a child in the home for unwed mothers. The lesson may not materialize until real love is found and the past rises up to threaten all chances for happiness.

The young boy who is taught not to steal may not learn his lesson until years later when indicted for embezzlement. Yet in one way or another, either by God's personal intervention or the operation of His morally constituted universe, we are forced to face the consequences of our actions. The result is usually some kind of suffering, whether physical pain, mental anguish, economic reversal, or the silent screams of a guilty conscience.

This section will look into the lives of some of the saints and sinners depicted in Holy Scripture. We gain profit from their lives because we have alongside the human events a divine commentary explaining the consequences and pinpointing the causes. While this study will not enable us to easily explain our own dilemmas, or assess for certain the role our own suffering is playing in God's scheme, it will provide us with a perspective by presenting the numerous roles suffering can play. The occasions in which we can explain with certainty the full story behind our sufferings will be rare. Sometimes our sufferings may play a combination of roles.

When Job's life fell apart, his so-called friends were certain he was suffering for his sins, that God was chastening him. We know Job's friends were wrong, but they did have a point. Some suffering is designed to teach us the importance of holy living and the utter devastation that always follows in the wake of sin.

DIRECT EDUCATION

King David presents a valuable case study. Since God quite clearly explains the consequences to David, through the prophet Nathan, we might term this direct education.

David's Misconception—David's problem lay in the idea that sin was serious for others, but not for himself. He could become incensed over a man with great herds feeding a guest the only ewe lamb of a poor neighbor (an account related by Nathan in order to awaken David to his sin), but had managed to remain quiet about his own affair with the beautiful wife of Uriah—an affair that produced a pregnancy that required the death of the soldier Uriah whose duties in battle clearly eliminated him as the father of the child.

How respectably David gave the secret orders to abandon Uriah on the field of battle, making death certain. How compassionately David took the grieving widow into his own household. After all, David was king. Such things were done by kings all the time.

Many men who aren't kings have often felt their own sins were a matter of personal privilege. When David, prodded by Nathan's parable (II Sam. 12:1-7), is forced to face his sin, he is told of the devastating harvest that awaits him. The child to be born of Bathsheba will die (II Sam. 12:14). David's family is to live in conflict: "The sword shall never depart from thine house," proclaims Nathan. From David's own sons will come rebellion (II Sam. 12:11) and murder.

How soon the harvest begins. The baby dies. David's son Amnon ravishes his own sister, Tamar. How can David rebuke him, in light of the affair with Bathsheba?

Another son, Absalom, executes revenge by murdering Amnon. How can David deal with such ruthlessness when Uriah's blood is on his hands? You can imagine the disrespect with which David's children viewed their father.

In a matter of years, Absalom undermines David and rises up in outright revolt, forcing David to flee for his life. As David's forces put down the rebellion, they slay Absalom. David's heart is broken and he cries out: "Would God I had died for thee, O Absalom, my son, my son!" (II Sam. 18:33).

Even as David lies dying, another son, Adonijah, revolts in an effort to be the new king in place of the appointed Solomon. And so a third son, Adonijah, is executed by a fourth son, Solomon. All of this comes as the consequence of a secret, illicit affair.

We do not have to guess at the anguish of heart experienced by David when at last he faced his sin. A study of Psalm 51 opens up his heart and lets us view the guilt-wrought turmoil. The throne on which he sits has become a pauper's bench, the crown on his head sets as lightly as a dunce cap. The scepter in his hand reminds only of the limitation of human power.

David's lesson —That David learns an eternal lesson is evident. He discovers that his own sins are serious and far-reaching. Your sins do find you out. We have but to read Psalm 51 to hear David's heartbeat. It reads like a secret diary penned in the author's own blood. King David has all the outward ingredients for happiness, yet he stands robbed of contentment. He commands a throne and a kingdom, yet stands crying like a deserted beggar. Every desire of his heart has been granted, but because his desire exceeded the bounds of God's holy law, he is possessed with emptiness.

He no longer thrills at the thought of God. Yet somehow he is not able to chase the thought from his mind. His subjects follow him, but God has deserted him. He has come to the place where multitudes still stand. Oscar Wilde spoke for many when he said: "I can resist everything except temptation."[2]

Sir Oliver Lodge once said: "We are like dogs at a picture gallery, only interested in smells and corners." Yet sooner or later we, like David, realize that our present world has no future. Christ keeps coming to our conscience and crying out: "My kingdom is not of this world."[3]

David learns that the loss of a clear conscience is the greatest of all losses. He wants to feel clean on the inside again: "Create in me a clean heart, O God" (Ps. 51:10). When David begs for the creation of a clean heart, he uses words found in the creation story of Genesis. The cleansing of a man's heart is no small task.

David discovers that pretense at last plays out. His first approach toward his sin was to pretend it didn't exist. No doubt he adopted a spirit of self-righteousness that enabled him to dwell on the sins of others. The church member who has drifted far from God often becomes the most self-righteous person in the community, easily observing the most minute flaws in other lives.

Alan Paton, in his book *Instrument of Thy Peace*, tells of a rabbi, a cantor, and a humble synagogue cleaner who are preparing for the Day of Atonement. While beating his breast, the rabbi said: "I am nothing; I am nothing." The cantor did likewise. However, when the cleaner beat his breast and said: "I am nothing," the rabbi was overheard to say to the cantor: "Look who thinks he's nothing."[4]

David, recognizing his attitude has been amiss, cries:

"Renew a right spirit within me" (Ps. 51:10). He wants God to be present in a way he can once more enjoy: "Restore unto me the joy of thy salvation" (Ps. 51:12). In the process of fulfilling his lusts, David has lost his happiness. His inner peace is gone. The most difficult lesson man has to learn is that material possessions have no power to bring happiness. Dr. Sangster once said with great irony: "America has more things than any other nation—and more books on how to find happiness!"[5]

Man is so accustomed to using monetary power as a means of making things right with those whom he has wronged, but he often feels completely frustrated when confronted with the problem of placating God. David realizes his great wealth will be no help at this point: "For thou desirest not sacrifice; else would I give it; thou delightest not in burnt offering" (Ps. 51:16).

We often think that prayer is the ready-made answer to every problem but there are times when prayer is to no avail. David could have prayed for the return of the joy of his salvation until doomsday and would never have obtained it. Churches are full of people praying for various and sundry things without any possibility of their prayers being answered. The problem is that they are not praying about the right thing. For instance, it is a waste for a drunk to pray for release from his hangover headaches. What he needs to pray about is the power to stop drinking. There are many people praying to be healed of physical ailments and mental anguish which are actually the results of their inner hatred and conflict toward other people. The source of their problem is never mentioned in their prayers. The medical profession is coming to realize that bitterness and hatred are the cause of many serious physical illnesses. In Ibsen's "Peer Gynt," the superintendent of the insane asylum says:

> It's here that men are most themselves—
> Themselves and nothing but themselves,
> Sailing with the outspread sails of self.
> Each shuts himself in a cask of self—

The cask stopped with a bung of self,
And seasoned in a well of self. None has a tear for other's woes, or cares what anyone thinks.[6]

There is no point in David praying until he is willing to confess his sins. The joy he seeks comes only through forgiveness, and forgiveness is predicated upon genuine confession of sins: "He that covereth his sins shall not prosper: but whoso confesseth and forsaketh them shall have mercy" (Prov. 28:13).

A part of the lesson David has to learn about the seriousness of sin involves the fact that forgiveness does not come as easily as some people suppose, nor as quickly. God withholds the peace and forgiveness for which David pleads until the lesson has been learned. God's approach to dealing with sin is to kill it. Real confession desires the eradication of the sin that has made life miserable. God's mercy comes to us as a cobalt machine and we must point out the place of the malignancy. When David cries: "Purge me" (Ps. 51:7), he is literally saying, "Unsin me."

In the New Testament (I John 1:9), there is a word used to describe the cleansing of a heart from sin that is often found in the papyri when speaking of a document that has been corrected by the removal of all errors. Certain corrections in our life have to be be made according to God's holy standard. David is tired of living with this portrait of sin etched on his conscience. The grave of Bathsheba's child is a constant reminder of his trangression. Day by day the turmoil within his own family reminds him that the sword indeed will never depart from his household. The lesson is sinking in. He realizes that sins do matter because they separate a man from God. Any wrongdoing is an affront to the heavenly Father. At last David cries out: "Against thee, thee only, have I sinned." He is not implying that his sin was not also against others. But he is recognizing that any sin is ultimately against God. As king, he supposed he had a right to do certain things, but he discovered that God is not remotely interested in what we think we have a right to do.

God is not some divine bellboy who brings joy to spiritual bums in order that they may enjoy peace of mind and untroubled sleep. God is in the business of remaking lives in order for men to find joy in serving Him. Unless a man's desire for cleansing carries with it a desire to be useful in God's kingdom, his motive is wrong. The man who desires to be free of the burden of guilt but who does not desire to take up the burden of responsibility is not yet finished with his confession. David discovers the right motive at last: "Then will I teach transgressors thy way; and sinners shall be converted unto thee" (Ps. 51:13).

David's sin was openly immoral. Yet it separated him no further from God than do the sins we sometimes refer to as respectable. The Bible pictures every sin as a deliberate rebellion against God growing out of a basic failure to believe all that God has revealed to us about ourselves and about morality. Dishonesty in business, however you may seek to justify it, will separate you from God just as surely as murder or adultery. Anyone who thinks otherwise still stands in need of divine education.

Now for a moment of reflection. We have looked at David's experience in an effort to see God's direct intervention to chasten David in such a way that he will learn a valuable lesson. The direction David had taken would ultimately have ruined him. If we feel that the chastisement was severe, it is because we have no way of knowing what would have happened apart from God caring enough to intervene.

However, we must also recognize that while God uses the prophet Nathan to explain to David all that is to come to pass as a result of David's sin, this does not necessarily mean that God caused it. It may just as well mean that God is explaining to David the devastation which quite naturally follows immoral living. We cannot be certain that God decreed the death of Bathsheba's baby. It is quite possible that God is merely explaining to David that his sin resulted in an illegitimate birth, and that the child itself would soon die. God may merely be explaining to David that his careless living will make such an impression upon his family that the sword will never depart from their midst. David's children will be so injured by the sin of their father that they themselves will throw all decency overboard. As their hypocritical father seeks to correct them, they will merely learn to hate him, and eventually to rebel against him. The point I am trying to make is that we are never quite able to discern just how much God personally intervenes, and just how much of our chastisement is a result of our own flaunting of basic moral laws with which our own souls have been constituted. We cannot be certain whether God was merely telling David to take a close look and observe the destruction that lies strewn in the wake of his sin, or whether God did indeed cause the death of the baby together with the resultant years of turmoil.

INDIRECT EDUCATION

Since it is very unlikely that any of us will have the benefit of God's personal commentary to explain the experiences of suffering that are designed to educate us, it is well to take a brief look at another Biblical experience where such commentary was not available to the person involved. I refer to the well-known story of the Prodigal Son (Luke 15). The story is a simple one. A young man decides he wants to leave home and go it on his own. He is tired of rules and authority. He is tired of a world full of dull people who have never had the backbone to go out and really live. Demanding his share of the inheritance, he departs the boring life of his home and sets out into the bright and glittering world.

The Prodigal's Misconception —It is not difficult to imagine the family quarrel that took place as the father sought to reason with the rebellious son. The prodigal's misconception is a simple one. No doubt he stated it emphatically to his father: "It's my business what I do with my life!" This sounds like a reasonable statement, outwardly. Shouldn't a person be able to do what he wants with his own life? When he comes of age, shouldn't he be allowed to do as he pleases? Tired of the everlasting "Thou shalt nots," the prodigal is determined to find his freedom. What he does not realize is that his own father desires that he have freedom. The difference comes over the definition of freedom. For the prodigal, freedom carried the idea of being beyond all rules and authority. He wanted to be away from the father's parental guidance. The father wants the son to be free from the entangling forces of sin so that he can find a full life. I think it was Luther who said: "Our human life is a battlefield between two masters. It is the question of being a child of one or a slave of the other."

With his pockets full of the father's inheritance (he never paused to consider this fact) the prodigal sets out into the world to live it up. What a time he must have had to begin with. The fat billfold draws many friends and good times are easy to have. He enjoys the company of harlots and the warmth of liquor. But alas, his money at last is gone and the time of harvest arrives. The land is filled with famine and he has nothing to eat. The wages of the "far country" begin to be seen for what they are. The only job available is that of feeding swine, and with the Jewish concept of the uncleanness of swine, this is the lowest job on the totem pole. He finds himself eating what the swine eat. His freedom has been short lived.

The Scripture tells us that at last "he came to himself." He began to remember what his life had been at home, under the father's authority.

The Prodigal's Lesson —Over a period of months the morally constituted universe in which we live was able to give sight to the blind prodigal. At last he began to see life more realistically. His education had been akin to that of the poor grass cutter who found a beautiful stone in the jungle. Assuming it to be a diamond, he took it to the jeweler's shop and displayed it with great delight. Being a kind and sympathetic man, the jeweler saw that if he were to tell the grass cutter that the stone was not a diamond, either the grass cutter would not believe it, or the shock of seeing his hopes dashed would bring him to despair. The jeweler therefore made plans to enable the poor man to discover his mistake for himself. The jeweler gave him work in his shop and kept him there until he began to distinguish the varieties of diamonds and their prices. Only then did the jeweler ask him to bring his stone back to the shop. Taking the stone from the carefully hidden box in his house, the grass cutter brought it to the store and laid it beside the real diamonds. To his amazement he realized the stone was worthless. Pale of face, he fell at the feet of his kind master and thanked him for his sympathetic goodness. He thanked him for not destroying his hope but rather making it possible for him to learn for himself. The grass cutter pledged to spend the rest of his life in the service of the kind jeweler. The heavenly Father sometimes uses similar procedures to help us find the truth when we have wandered away from Him. Once we discover it, if we have any character about us, we will determine to follow such a caring Father.[7]

Realizing that the only time in his life when life had meant anything was that time spent with his father, the young man decides to return and confess his sin, asking the father's forgiveness. There is something very healing in the experience wherein a man finds that he is nothing apart from the Father's mercy. God created man out of the dust of the earth, and He cares enough to continue to remake man, to salvage him out of the ruin of his own mistakes and wasted capacities.

The prodigal who supposed that what he did was his own business, at last discovers that it is also the heavenly Father's business. The Scripture reminds us that "no man liveth unto himself, and no man dieth unto himself." Everything we do affects others, and affects the heavenly Father. Since we are God's handiwork, we can never assume that our choices are our own business. Since loved ones are affected by what we do, we can never assume that we live in solitary confinement. The mere fact that we are part of the human race makes everything we do everyone else's business. This young man had discovered the truth expressed by the apostle Paul who said: "All things are lawful unto me, but all things are not expedient; all things are lawful for me, but I will not be brought under the power of any" (I Cor. 6:12). The word *expedient* carries the concept of being able to walk around and carry your own weight. Everything you do will not bear its own weight, will not support itself. Rather many things burden you down like parasites. The prodigal slammed the door on life and walked away toward death. In the land of the spiritually dead he at last came to his senses and returned to the father's home where he had found life.

God must either allow us to grow up like a spoiled child who has never been denied anything, or He must care about us enough to chasten us for our education. We have looked at two men—a proud king and a wayward son. Each man learned some things he needed to learn. Yet God did not deal with these men merely for the benefit of their own correction. Each one stands as an object lesson for all the world. We have the option of learning from their suffering rather than having to learn from our own. God explains the circumstances surrounding the lives of these two men for our benefit. Neither of these men had to learn anything from their experiences. They could have remained in rebellion and learned nothing. We have the same option. You can force a child to go to school, but you cannot force him to learn anything. Some children wait out the years of schooling, determined never to study and never to learn.

The law of God is summed up in Jesus Christ, God's fullest revelation to us. The problems we think we have are not our real problems. Our first problem is Jesus

Christ. In an age that clamors for freedom, we must realize that man's only freedom, where God is concerned, is the freedom to say yes or no. We are never free to avoid answering at all. Beset by his own sins, man lives in misery. With God's help, however, he can see the error of his way and come back to life. The misery can become grandeur.

NOTES

1. Robert Browning Hamilton, quoted by T. B. Maston, *Suffering, A Personal Perspective* (Nashville: Broadman Press, 1967), p. 65.
2. George Buttrick (ed.), *Interpreter's Bible* (New York: Abingdon Press, 1952), Vol. I, p. 506.
3. *Pulpit Digest* (February 1969), p. 33.
4. *Pulpit Digest* (May 1968), p. 59.
5. *Pulpit Digest* (February 1969), p. 39.
6. Henrik Ibsen, *Peer Gynt,* Act IV, Scene XIII (New York: Dutton, Everyman's Library Edition), p. 163.
7. James Hastings (ed.), *The Speaker's Bible* (Grand Rapids: Baker Book House, 1962), Vol. III, p. 15.

6

Suffering That Contributes to Spiritual Growth

"And he said unto me, My grace is sufficient for thee: for my strength is made perfect in weakness. Most gladly therefore will I rather glory in my infirmities, that the power of Christ may rest upon me" (II Cor. 12:9).

Suffering can enhance spiritual growth. At first glance, suffering that educates (as discussed in the previous chapter) may seem to be identical with the present discussion. There is one major distinction. Suffering as a means of education has to do with God's chastisement of us because of our sins, our wrong choices, in an effort to redirect us. We now turn to examine suffering that has nothing to do with chastisement. Sometimes God allows us to suffer because it provides an opportunity for character-building, for expansion of our spiritual dimension.

Our discussion will focus on the apostle Paul. Take a look at his travelogue. He was publicly beaten, five times with leather thongs and three times with clubs. He was stoned and left for dead. Three times he was shipwrecked. Often he had narrow escapes from highwaymen seeking to rob him. On numerous occasions he was betrayed by his native countrymen and pursued by the heathen to whom he sought to bring salvation. Many times he went to bed hungry and thirsty. Cold winter winds often chilled his ill-clad body. The small congregations which he established were constantly calling on him to help them straighten out misunderstandings and breaches in the fellowships. The burden of their problems weighed heavily upon him. Sometimes they even turned on him as though he were a charlatan. Besides all of this his health was bad. One particular malady was so severe that it often incapacitated him. He does not tell us the nature of the disease, but merely refers to it as his "thorn in the flesh." The word translated "thorn" was in reality a sharp wooden stake on which criminals were impaled as a means of execution. This was Paul's way of explaining that his illness was chronic. Like a stake jostling in his side, constantly causing festering and pain, his disease was ever present (II Cor. 11:24–12:10).

None of these painful experiences are present as chastisement. Paul was faithful in every area of life. His commitment was total. He had left a prestigious position in Judaism. He stayed on the road constantly in an effort to preach the gospel to the whole world. He held nothing back from God. Yet he suffered. We do not have to ask why God allowed it. Paul tells us. Though speaking directly of his thorn, he no doubt includes all his suffering in the explanation: "And he said unto me, My grace is sufficient for thee, for my strength is made perfect in weakness. Most gladly therefore will I rather glory in my infirmities, that the power of Christ may rest upon me" (II Cor. 12:9).

What an amazing affirmation! Paul is actually giving thanks for his sufferings. You see, he understands that a soldier is never really a soldier until he has been through a battle. Faith never grows much until it has nothing to stand on except God's promises. Thanksgiving is never real until a man has learned to be thankful when the cupboard is bare, when health is gone, when the sun is hidden.

Centuries before Paul, another man had made the same discovery. The prophet Habakkuk, living in the midst of hardship, affirmed: "Although the fig tree shall not blossom, neither shall fruit be in the vines; the labour of the olive shall fail, and the fields shall yield no meat; the flock shall be cut off from the fold, and there shall be no herd in the stalls: yet I will rejoice in the

Lord, I will joy in the God of my salvation. The Lord God is my strength" (Hab. 3:17-19a).

When faced in the stance of faith, there is a note of music in suffering. The strings of a violin remain silent until put into use. Even then, their sound is dull unless stretched tight. Beyond that, lies the necessity of a skilled musician to call forth the best harmony. The strings of our heart can be tightened by suffering, but only if the Master Musician is allowed to play those strings will there be heavenly music.[1]

A word of caution is necessary. Do not seek to impose suffering on yourself in an effort to become more spiritual. Others have fallen into such a pit. Self-inflicted suffering becomes a veiled form of pride and self-glorification. The early church father, Ignatius, is a case in point. He was not content until arrested by Imperial Rome and seemed eager to be thrown to the lions, believing his martyrdom would somehow enhance his standing with God. While en route to Rome as a prisoner he wrote letters of rejoicing as though he were traveling toward a coronation.

A century later, Origen of Alexandria emasculated himself thinking that this would make his discipleship certain, supposing Jesus intended His words to be taken literally when He said that some "have made themselves eunuchs for the kingdom of heaven's sake" (Matt. 19:12).

Henry Susa, a German mystic of the fourteenth century, and an advocate of the "cult of pain," is said to have worn between his shoulders a cross containing iron nails pressing against his flesh. His shirt was made of horsehair and contained straps implanted with five hundred sharp points. He wore gloves inside of which were pins projected against his hands. He often beat himself until the blood flowed. All of this he did because he believed that suffering bestowed something sacred upon the sufferer.[2]

Suffering in itself has no value. We should not seek it nor enjoy it. Self-induced suffering becomes an instrument of Satan to produce spiritual pride. Yet when we cannot escape suffering, we can rejoice in the knowledge that God has the power to use even suffering to accomplish spiritual growth. "All things work together for good" (Rom. 8:28) is a Scriptural cliche seldom understood aright. My own translation reads: "We know that God is able to bring good out of any circumstance in the lives of those who love him." The problem comes at the point of our definition of "good." We equate "good" with health, prosperity, luxury. God equates "good" with being "conformed to the image of his Son" (Rom. 8:29). Suffering, when both the pain and the pained are yielded to God, can mold Christian character.

We are to understand that God does not cause everything to happen. Human choices, both our own and those about us, enter into the picture. Not everything that happens is good, but God has the power to use anything, however bad, to make us more Christlike.[3]

Dr. Harry Emerson Fosdick reminds us that our human vocabulary would be impoverished were it not for words like "grief" and "calamity," for then we would have no words like "bravery" and "fortitude."[4] The painful experiences keep us aware of what is important, lest we conform to Bishop Frances Asbury's caricature as he said, "Never have I seen any people who would talk so long, so correctly, and so seriously about trifles."[5]

GROWTH IN HUMILITY

Now back to Paul. He shares with us his awareness that his sufferings were playing a vital role. They were delivering him from spiritual pride. His conversion on the Damascus road had delivered him from the pride of Phariseeism grounded in the good works of legalism. He had learned to trust totally in Christ for salvation.

Now he faces a different kind of pride, the pride of pietism. He had a rich inner life. He had experienced moments of spiritual ecstasy in which he had seen heavenly visions. The thorn, together with his other sufferings, became the means of delivering him from pietistic pride: "And lest I should be exalted above measure through the abundance of revelations, there was given to me a thorn in the flesh" (II Cor. 12:7).

Paul tells us it would have been easy to brag about his inner experiences, to glory in them. Yet he realizes that to do so would be to glorify himself (II Cor. 12:5-6). While he would not take anything for his mystical experiences, he recognizes that it has been his hardships that have produced spiritual growth. Indeed, his visions could cause much harm by robbing him of humility. The thorn makes humility possible.

The times when adversity was the greatest, when death seemed certain, were times that humbly reminded him of his mortality. In discussing such experiences he says: "We had the sentence of death in ourselves" (II Cor. 1:9a). The idea is that of a verdict or judgment: "We realized that our verdict was death, and that realization remains with us until now." This verdict, being indigenous to our frailty, has a part to play: "That we should not trust in ourselves, but in God which raiseth the dead" (II Cor. 1:9b).

An old Chinese proverb says: "Of the thirty-six ways of avoiding disaster, running away is best." But sometimes there is nowhere to run. We pride ourselves on our resourcefulness, our ingenuity, but when there is no way out, no escape from pain and danger, we learn humility.

GROWTH IN SPIRITUAL INSIGHT

André Gide tells the story of a lovely girl who had been blind since birth. Naturally her blindness had provided her with a rather sheltered, limited life. When she suddenly received her sight by means of surgery, she was impressed by two things. First, she could not believe how beautiful the world of nature was. Second, she noticed the sadness that marked so many faces. Those furrowed brows of anxiety almost made her wish her sight had not been restored.[6] Sadness is universal, but sometimes sadness itself becomes the surgery that brings sight.

It was so with Paul. He saw life more realistically through the tears of his thorn. He is saying, "It helps me keep my feet on the ground" (II Cor. 12:7: "Lest I be exalted above measure").[7] Although disease is a part of the evil wrought by Satan ("the messenger of Satan," II Cor. 12:7), God has the power to use malady to heighten spiritual insight.

Robert Louis Stevenson, a man gifted in literary talents, was handicapped by tuberculosis which would ultimately take his life at the age of forty-four. Yet he pursued his dreams. When his right hand failed, he learned to write with his left. When this failed, he dictated his works. When his voice failed, he used the sign language of the deaf and dumb to dictate a novel. This is the man who wrote, "This world is so full of a number of things, I am sure we should all be as happy as kings."[8]

Someone has suggested that "disappointment is like a sieve. Through its coarse meshes small ambitions and hopes and endeavors of the soul are sifted out relentlessly. But the things that are big enough not to fall through are not in the least affected by it. It is only a test, not a finality."[9]

The easy, carefree life does little to help us see clearly. Over the doorway of the cathedral at Milan are three inscriptions spanning the arches. Upon one arch is carved a wreath of roses and underneath is the sentence: "All that pleases is but for a moment." Over the second is carved a cross with the words: "All that troubles is but for a moment." On the third arch is the legend: "That only is important which is eternal."[10] Sometimes the thorns force us to sort out the eternal. Paul himself explains this process: "We look not at the things which are seen, but the things which are not seen: for the things which are seen are temporal; but the things which are not seen are eternal" (II Cor. 4:18).

GROWTH IN DEPENDENCE ON GOD

Paul tells us there were three separate times when he prayed to be healed from his chronic illness (II Cor.

12:8). Although Paul was faithfully committed to God, God's answer was a promise, not a miracle: "And he said unto me, My grace is sufficient for thee: for my strength is made perfect in weakness'" (II Cor. 12:9). God's answer was: "You will have to depend on the strength of my presence to help you bear the pain." In this context, God's grace is the gift of His presence. Our strength must come from the knowledge that He shares our suffering with us.

Dostoevski, the great Russian writer of the nineteenth century, tells of being in solitary confinement because of his political opinions. Each evening a little shutter in his cell door was opened and an anonymous voice whispered, "Courage, brother, we also suffer." In much the same way Christ whispers encouragement to us. We rest in the assurance that God is able to add another chapter to every situation. The world never has the last say.

During Paul's imprisonment at Rome, when he needed help and encouragement in the worst way, he sadly writes to Timothy: "All men forsook me." However, in this experience of loneliness he goes on to say: "Notwithstanding the Lord stood with me, and strengthened me" (II Tim. 4:16-17).

In the New Testament, the word "manifold" means "many-colored." In his First Epistle, Simon Peter uses the word only twice. The first time he uses the word to describe trials—they come in all colors (I Peter 1:6). The second usage describes God's grace (I Peter 4:10). It also comes in all colors. What a beautiful picture. There is a grace for every trial, tailor-made for every trial. Thus a John Milton can write poetry while blind and a Beethoven can compose though living in the silent world of deafness because God's grace is sufficient. In those times when we come to the end of our rope, when only God is left to depend on, we grow spiritually. Only weakness allows power to fulfill itself. It is difficult to help the strong. What can you give to the wealthy? Pain can bring us to depend on the overshadowing presence of Christ if it shows us our bankruptcy: "And he said unto me, My grace is sufficient for thee: for my strength is made perfect in weakness."

GROWTH IN MINISTERING TO OTHERS

Whether or not we live a victorious life is dependent on whether we become a prisoner of circumstances or a user of them. From a Roman prison, Paul writes: "I would have you understand, brethren, that the things which happened unto me have fallen out rather unto the furtherance of the gospel" (Phil. 1:12). Being guarded by the choicest of Caesar's palace soldiers allowed a unique opportunity for witness to them.

There are times when the ratio of our opportunity is akin to the ratio of our suffering. Some doors are opened only by pain. God calls us to His side, not to free us from all conflict, but to strengthen us for battle. Paul explains: "For as the sufferings of Christ abound in us, so our consolation [comfort] also aboundeth by Christ" (II Cor. 1:5). Only as we have been comforted by God, in the midst of trial, are we able to share that comfort with others. Concerning God, Paul writes: "Who comforteth us in all our tribulation, that we may be able to comfort them which are in any trouble, by the comfort wherewith we ourselves are comforted of God" (II Cor. 1:4).

Pain is a part of our on-the-job training. It allows us to share the suffering of others by virtue of having walked the path before. We live in a world of frustration that could be identified with Stephen Leacock's famous rider who "flung himself upon his horse and rode off madly in all directions." Many share the uncertainty of Edna St. Vincent Millay who said, "Life must go on, but I forget just why."[11] In this kind of world, there is much need for someone who can answer such "whys," for someone who can explain that you need not suffer alone, but that Christ offers to suffer with you. Not only that, but Christ also offers to share with you His eternal glory (Rom. 8:16-17).

Paul's opportunity for witness came in jail cells and busy marketplaces. Yours may come in a hospital bed. Viktor Frankl, the noted psychiatrist, endured the horrors of Hitler's concentration camps. In telling of his experiences he noted that some men in the camp came to believe all opportunities for life had passed. These men simply vegetated and slowly died. A few were able to see a challenge in their dread experiences by seeing the possibility of an inner triumph over the outward circumstances and thus found meaning and kept alive a desire to live.[12]

Winifred Holtly, a gifted writer, was told at the age of thirty-two that she had only a few more years to live. Her spirit rebelled against the fate that cut short her ambitions. Beset by depression, she was walking in the country one cold winter day and came across a water trough. Seeing some thirsty lambs, she took her walking stick and broke the ice allowing the lambs to drink. Vera Brittain, who tells the story, says at the moment Winifred broke the ice she heard a voice from within saying, "Having nothing, yet possessing all things." The voice was so distinct that she looked around to see who had spoken. No one was there. In that moment her bitterness was gone, together with her ambitions for personal glory and accomplishment. She spoke of the event as her "moment of conversion." Until her death at the age of thirty-seven, she associated her experience with the words of Bernard Bosanquet on salvation: "And now we are saved absolutely, we need not say from what, we are at home in the universe, and, in principle and in the main, feeble and timid creatures as we are, there is nothing anywhere within the world or without it that can make us afraid."[13]

Pain is an ugly guest whom we fear, and yet whom we cannot lock out. Yet when he is gone, we sometimes find he was a friend who left behind a rich treasure.

George Matheson, noted poet and man of God, lost his sight as a youth and spent forty years in darkness. The third stanza of one of his widely known songs reads:

> O Joy that seekest me through pain,
> I cannot close my heart to thee;
> I trace the rainbow through the rain,
> And feel the promise is not vain
> That morn shall tearless be.

He had learned to live with his darkness. More than that, he had learned to be benefited by his handicap. His victory is seen in the words he once wrote:

> My God, I have never thanked thee for my thorn. I have thanked thee one thousand times for my roses, but never once for my thorn. I have been looking forward to a world where I shall get compensation for my cross, but I never thought of my cross as a present glory. Teach me the glory of my cross. Teach me the the value of my thorn. Show me that I have climbed to Thee by the path of pain. Show me that my tears have been my rainbow.[14]

Paul had not only learned much from his thorn, but had grown much because of it. Therefore he could say, "I am able to see good in my sickness, my insults, my hardships, and my persecutions" (II Cor. 12:10, translation mine).

Paul was a better Christian because of his sufferings. His faith was stronger and vision clearer because of them. Somehow his hardships make more meaningful his closing words to Timothy: "I have fought a good fight, I have finished my course, I have kept the faith" (II Tim. 4:7).

NOTES

1. T. B. Maston, *Suffering, A Personal Perspective* (Nashville: Broadman Press, 1967), p. 68.
2. Merrill Proudfoot, *Suffering: A Christian Understanding* (Philadelphia: The Westminster Press, 1964), pp. 137-41.
3. For a fuller discussion, see my book, *God's Answer to Anxiety* (Nashville: Broadman Press, 1968), pp. 27-34.
4. Harry E. Fosdick, *The Secret of Victorious Living* (New York: Harper and Row, Publishers, 1934), p. 14.
5. *Pulpit Digest* (July-August 1968), p. 50.
6. *Pulpit Digest* (November 1970), p. 43.
7. B. W. Woods, *God's Answer to Anxiety,* p. 44.
8. *Christianity Today* (December 5, 1969), p. 15.
9. Clarence E. Macartney, *Macartney's Illustrations* (Nashville: Abingdon Press, 1945), p. 98.
10. Ibid., pp. 352-53.
11. *Pulpit Digest* (November 1970), pp. 43-44.
12. Viktor E. Frankl, *Man's Search for Meaning* (New York: Washington Square Press, Inc., 1963), p. 115.
13. Leslie Weatherhead, *Prescription for Anxiety* (Nashville: Abingdon Press), pp. 133-34, quoting *Testament of Friendship* (The Macmillan Co., 1940), p. 325.
14. *Christianity Today* (November 8, 1963), p. 54.

7

Suffering That Proves the Reality of Faith

"Doth Job fear God for nought?" (Job 1:9).

Rabbi Elazar ben Pedat once comforted another rabbi in the grip of illness by explaining his suffering in terms of a man who had two cows. If a burden must be placed on one of the cows, the owner will choose to place it on the stronger cow. So, Rabbi Elazar reasoned, God tries only the righteous because the wicked could not endure it.[1]

The simple analogy prepares the setting for the suffering of Job. By means of divine revelation we are allowed to eavesdrop on a conversation between God, the giver of life, and Satan, the perverter of life. When confronted by the apparent faithfulness of Job, Satan cynically retorts: "You don't think Job serves You without expecting to be repaid, do You?" (paraphrase mine). The Septuagint translation: "Doth Job fear God for nothing?" uses a word (translated "nothing") that in the noun form means "gift." Used abverbially here, the idea is that of doing something freely, without thought of recompense. Satan believes Job's piety is the height of self-interest. Job is accused of serving God because it pays dividends, rather than serving Him out of a faith based on love.

Satan is very crafty. It is impossible to serve God without being repaid. The good life is in itself a reward. Heaven is a land of rewards, an inheritance prepared for God's children. Still there is a distinction to be made between serving faithfully out of love, and serving selfishly for a share of the inheritance. The particular area involved here seems to deal with earthly compensation. Satan contends that Job is faithful because God has bought him off with material riches.

Hence we recognize another possible role for suffering —we may be allowed to suffer in order to prove that our faith is not born out of the belief that the godly life puts more money in the bank and more laughter in the home. We may be allowed to suffer so that our faith can be verified as going deeper than earthly blessings, as not dependent on the presence of ease and prosperity.

Since Job represents a threat to the false philosophy of evil forces, Satan suggests a test. He requests permission to take from Job all the surrounding pleasures—his herds, his children, and his health. Only then, reasoned Satan, will we learn if Job's faith is genuine. God's willingness to allow such an ordeal was based on His assurance that Job's faith would stand victorious, like a lighthouse beacon on a stormy night. Here and there, in the annals of the human story, there must be strong men whose suffering points others to divine strength. Job, without being asked, or warned, is thrust into a milieu of grief and pain that he might emerge as God's answer to all cynics who believe that every man has his price.

FAITH REQUIRES NO SET CIRCUMSTANCES

No doubt Job could have written quite a success story. He is described as "the greatest of all the men of the east" (Job 1:3c). Not only did he have prosperity, but also a house full of children—seven sons and three daughters. Both wealth and children were considered as signs of divine favor in those days. The Hebrews assumed that the good life guaranteed health and prosperity while the evil life led to poverty and sickness. Somehow God had to show them that sometimes the innocent suffer, that sometimes the faithful lose everything. Job himself needed to have this important insight. We may well wonder just how near Job really was to being guilty of Satan's accusation. Job does seem to have shared God's opinion: "And the Lord said unto Satan,

Hast thou considered my servant Job, that there is none like him in the earth, a perfect and an upright man, one that feareth God, and escheweth evil?" (Job 1:8). Job was realistic enough to know that he was living a good life before the Lord. The sudden reversal in his fortunes was hard to explain within the bounds of the theology of his day.

Satan's challenge was: "Hast thou not made an hedge about him, and about his house, and . . . hast blessed the work of his hands. . . . But put forth thine hand now, and touch all that he hath, and he will curse thee to thy face" (Job 1:10-11).

Yet Job, though confused and depressed, does not lose his faith. When all was well, he had faithfully worshiped God. His concern for the spiritual welfare of his children had led him to offer prayers and sacrifices daily in their behalf, saying, "It may be that my sons have sinned and cursed God in their hearts" (Job 1:5).

In the wake of catastrophe, with the pieces of his shattered world lying scattered, with funeral wreaths on the door and bankruptcy notices in the paper, "Job arose, and rent his mantle, and shaved his head, and fell down upon the ground, and worshipped" (Job 1:20).

Though totally bewildered and stunned, his faith remains. He worships! His daily devotions are not dependent on his earthly circumstances. Here lies the real test of faith. Dare we honestly put our own devotion to such a test? When the smelting fires of suffering burn away all the dross, what is left is genuine. Pulitzer Prize winning correspondent Harrison E. Salisbury, a foremost authority on the Soviet Union, tells of not only the survival, but the growth of the Russian church and explains these phenomena in terms of the church's deep spiritual roots coupled with a faith that has been purified by much suffering.[2]

FAITH THAT GOD ALONE IS WORTH FOLLOWING

The test of genuine faith is whether God, in Himself,

is sufficient reason for remaining faithful. We look upon Job in a time when God was all he had left. As he and his wife sit alone in an earth as silent as a mausoleum, he can no longer be accused of living a life exempt from the pain that all others suffer. Here is his supreme test. With what courage will he face the new day made empty by a cold sun?

Hear him: "Naked came I out of my mother's womb, and naked shall I return thither: the Lord gave, and the Lord hath taken away; blessed be the name of the Lord" (Job 1:21).

God is good —Do we hear aright? Is Job still claiming that God is good? He seems certain of this truth. He speaks of coming from, and returning to, his "mother's womb" much as we would speak of "mother earth." He has experienced life only because God has formed him from the dust of the earth, and to that dust he shall someday return. Therefore he thanks God for the gift of life, even when as brief as the lives of his children. He refuses to attack God's character: "In all this Job sinned not, nor charged God foolishly" (Job 1:22). Amidst death and loss, continued faith cannot be refuted. Such faith is its own proof.

God is sufficient—We hear no talk of being deserted. Job still believes God is enough! When sudden winds of adversity snatch from a man his living memorial, his children, and health is gone so that one's death seems near, all hope of remembrance is bound up in God.

Several years ago a missionary on the island of Formosa lost his wife by a terrible disease. Six weeks later the malady snatched from him his fifteen-year-old son. The natives to whom he had preached watched his every move. They saw him walk to the grave in a quiet and stately manner. They sensed in his grief a note of hope and victory. One was heard to say, "I do not know about his religion, or about the Christ he serves, but I do know that I like the way he buries his dead. There is a difference in his sorrow and ours. We shriek with horror and anguish. We have no hope. This man acts as if he knows where his dead loved ones are going."

FAITH'S VICTORY OVER SUFFERING

When a man loses everything, does he turn to the world in bitterness? Does he become a caged animal eager to strike out at anybody nearby? Not so if faith is real.

Rise above self-preservation —When the loss of family and wealth fails to vindicate Satan's prediction, he answers by saying Job's faith will not endure personal pain. Therefore Satan cries: "Skin for skin, yea, all that a man hath will he give for his life. But put forth thine hand now and touch his bone and his flesh, and he will curse thee to thy face" (Job 2:4-5).

Satan's accusation is that a man will do anything, say anything to save his hide. But Satan was wrong, wrong about Job and wrong about every martyr who has died rather than denounce his faith.

Accept God's sovereignty —The secret to a faith that rises above the instinct for self-preservation is a faith that accepts God's sovereignty. Real faith involves a surrender to God's purposes. When Job's wife taunts him by suggesting he give up his faith and curse God, he answers: "What, shall we receive good at the hand of God, and shall we not receive evil?" (Job 2:10).

I suspect that Job was not only preaching a sermon to his wife, but to himself as well. Every child of God finds himself, occasionally, in need of self-encouragement. He reminds us that we have no right to expect special treatment from God. If we accept the good, we must also be prepared to accept the bad.

Job could have cursed the thieves that took his herds, the storm that took his children, the boils which covered his body, or the God who stood by and let it all happen. Instead he bows to God's wisdom and providence. Somehow, he still has faith in God's justice. He still believes there will be a time when light will be cast on the dark path. He still trusts God.

Job's simple statement is another way of saying that God who gives air to breathe, eyes to see, a family to enjoy, the songs of birds to hear, can withdraw everything and yet take only what is His.

Though the substance of all of Job's hopes and dreams has been removed, he has faith to believe the shipwreck is not total. Yet we dare not suppose that all of this comes easy for Job. The following chapters of Job reveal that the struggle was difficult. Job was not patient in the current sense of the word. When the Bible refers to the "patience of Job" (James 5:11) we need to remember that the word thus translated means "to endure."

Job sets an example of endurance in these preliminary words to his wife, and later as his faith triumphs (Job 42:1-6). However, between these two points in his pilgrimage lie many questions. Job submits. He endures. But he does want to know why. He is frustrated. At times he is even angry. Who wouldn't be? Only a robot can live apart from human emotion. The point is, however, that he never stops believing. He never resigns from membership in God's family. Perhaps Stevenson catches something of the searching hope of Job as he writes:

> God, if this were enough,
> That I see things bare to the buff
> And up to the buttocks in mire;
> That I ask not hope nor hire,
> Nut in the husk,
> Nor dawn beyond the dusk,
> Nor life beyond death:
> God, if this were faith?

* * *

> To go on forever and fail and go on again,
> And be mauled to the earth and arise,
> And contend for the shade of a word and a thing not seen with the eyes:
> With the half of a broken hope for a pillow at night

That somehow the right is the right
And the smooth shall bloom from the rough:
Lord, if that were enough?[3]

Faith is the stance with which we offer up all of life to the heavenly Father. In our youth, we offer our fervent spirit. If strength be given us, we offer that; if weakness be our lot, we offer that. And if in God's grace we are allowed to grow old, we must give Him the wisdom and maturity that comes in the silver years. If by faith we praise Him amidst earthly joys, we can, by that same faith, praise Him amidst stifled sobs.

Genuine faith accepts the challenge of life in Christ's name. Our own strength and our own wisdom will fail. We have no easy answers to life's dilemmas, but we follow Him who is the master of every moment, the Lord of time and eternity.

I sat one day in the home of a fine young Christian mother who was fighting a losing battle with a brutal malignancy. As we talked of her coming death, and of the concern she had for her children, she expressed the normal fears and regrets. She too was beset by the "whys" of her fate, but as our conversation ended, she expressed a determination to die as a Christian ought to die. This is no small vocation. There are many aspects of the Christian witness. The world needs to be shown how to love, how to care, how to repent, and especially, how to die. This she did! When the final onslaught swept upon her, when fever burned her frail body and pain became one constant agony, in short, when the hurricane had swept all else away, there stood outlined against the dark sky, her faith, undisputed, unrelenting, unafraid. Her death was her moment of victory.

And so Satan is doomed to failure. James McKechnie, in discussing Job, elaborates upon this thought. Satan's gains are at the same time his losses. Satan "makes of Job a rebel, and in rebellion Job lays grip on a deeper loyalty. . . . Satan accomplishes nothing for God, though God may accomplish much through Satan."[4] Our heavenly Father deals in the miraculous, and can use even suffering to confute the arguments of evil and affirm the reality of our faith.

NOTES

1. C. J. G. Montefiore and H. M. J. Loewe (eds.), *A Rabbinic Anthology* (London: Macmillan and Co., Ltd., 1938), selection no. 1542.
2. Andrew W. Blackwood, Jr., *Devotional Introduction to Job* (Grand Rapids: Baker Book House, 1959), p. 23.
3. Robert Louis Stevenson, "If This Were Faith," in *Masterpieces of Religious Verse,* ed. James Dalton Morrison (New York: Harper & Bros. Publishers, 1948), p. 381, selection no. 1225.
4. James McKechnie, *Job, Moral Hero, Religious Egoist, and Mystic* (New York: George H. Doran Co., 1927), pp. 30-31.

8

Suffering That Reveals God

G. K. Chesterton once said: "You can define a book in this way. Boy and girl meet in the first chapter; boy and girl kiss in the last chapter; the book tells why it took so long."[1] Real life is not always so neatly ordered. There are many chapters that do not follow the usual romantic ending.

A young preacher took to himself a wife. They had the usual dreams akin to young couples. But gradually something began to happen. At first the husband could not believe anything was seriously wrong. He was a young man deeply grounded in his religious faith. He had approached the marriage prayerfully and had felt God's direction in the matter. Yet there remained the frightening suspicion that something was wrong. By the time their second child was born, the young preacher was almost certain his wife was seeing someone else. Shortly after the arrival of the third child, he was sure of it. The names given the last two children indicate the suspicion that tore at his heart. The second child's name meant literally, "the withdrawal of love," and the third child's name, "not my kin."

Recognizing the characters in this drama is not difficult. They are Hosea and Gomer. Though they lived in the eighth century B.C., their tragedy is terribly modern.

What a relief it would be if life could be perfectly ordered. Several years ago a baseball game was staged between the actors and the comedians in which Groucho Marx managed the comedians. Jack Benny was the first batter and Groucho ordered him to hit a home run. When Benny struck out, Groucho immediately resigned saying he would have no part of managing a team that wouldn't follow instructions.[2] Sometimes life doesn't follow instructions either, and dreams become nightmares.

In the experience of Hosea we find another example of the use which God can make of suffering. He is always able to salvage some good out of it when the person involved permits Him to be a part of the drama. The suffering in this instance is not physical pain but mental and emotional anguish which is probably the most severe of all suffering. The good which is salvaged from the experience is a deeper insight into God's character, particularly into God's love that offers forgiveness. After the heartbreak of Hosea, men would forever have a vivid picture of the depth of God's love.

THE AGONY

There are times when all marital advice fails. A famous star once said that she and her husband followed the practice of never going to sleep until all arguments were settled. She went on to confess that sometimes they went for days without any sleep. The final commentary on her secret to a successful marriage was pronounced by the divorce court.

Love betrayed —Perhaps no agony exceeds that of a betrayed heart. When conflict leads to suspicion, and suspicion becomes open reality, there seems to be nothing left. Jealousy, though a sin when nurtured by envious and selfish people or harbored by untrusting folks without cause, is a perfectly legitimate emotion in the heart of one who loves deeply, and sees the object of his love being given to someone else. A husband who can watch his wife give herself to someone else without being torn by jealousy has never known love. God said of Himself, as He gave the Ten Commandments: "I the Lord thy God am a jealous God" (Exod. 20:5). He said it in the context of the second commandment forbidding the worship of false gods. When love that has been pledged to God is then directed toward some other source of allegiance, God is jealous, and rightly so. He knows that such action will spell disaster for those involved. So it is with a husband or wife who sees his/her helpmate following a course of unfaithfulness that will destroy both the marriage and the life of the offender.

Love that is real is grounded in personal commitment. The marriage ceremony is designed to verbalize that commitment. The hippie philosophy of free love which, in an attempt to be open and broadminded, advocates the sharing of one's intimate love with others is in reality a confession of no love.

Hosea sees his wife begin a course that leads at last to adultery. She gives herself freely to others, without any semblance of respect for her commitment to Hosea, and without any commitment from her new lovers. She is not content with one affair but throws overboard all restraint. Leaving her husband and children, she becomes a woman of the streets.

Amidst anguish and torment, Hosea searches for reasons. He looks back on the time of their engagement and remembers how certain he had been that the marriage was within God's will. Now it seems that God led him to marry a harlot: "And the Lord said to Hosea, Go, take unto thee a wife of whoredoms and children of whoredoms: for the land hath committed great whoredom, departing from the Lord" (Hos. 1:2). True, Gomer's people were not religious, but she had seemed different. Now it seems that her course of action was destined to follow that of her people, and of the citizenry in general. Did God know all along how the marriage would end? If so, why did He permit Hosea to make such a mistake? These and a thousand other questions tore at Hosea's mind. How is he to face his friends, his family? How can he ever preach again? Should he even think of continuing his prophetic calling? If he could have resigned from the human race, he would have done so gladly. To have tried to convince him that anything good could be salvaged from the ruins of his home would have been impossible. To convince him that a deeper concept of God could arise from the ashes of his heart would have brought the empty laugh of absurdity. It is no wonder that scholars have observed disorganization in the Book of Hosea. It is the account of a man stumbling through the aftermath of a hurricane, his eyes blinded with tears and his heart torn out.

Love extended again —Just as Hosea was certain God had forsaken him, he hears Him speak in the inner voice of the soul: "Go again, love [the same] woman [Gomer] who is beloved as a paramour and is an adulteress, even as the Lord loves the children of Israel, though they turn to other gods and love cakes of raisins [used in the sacrificial feasts in idol worship]" (Hos. 3:1, The Amplified Old Testament).

I am sure Hosea was taken aback by such a thought. Pride does enter the picture. Can he take back a woman who has disgraced him? Can he forgive a woman who has flaunted his love? The difficulty of such a decision is evident in a conversation I had several years ago with a pastor-friend of mine. He mentioned a counseling appointment he had coming up later in the day with an estranged couple. The wife had been unfaithful. The pastor was trying to get the couple back together. I asked him, "What would you do if your wife was unfaithful to you?" He looked at me thoughtfully and then replied, "'I'd kill her." Similar thoughts no doubt coursed through Hosea's mind. Could he really love her again? Had his love been able to survive? The enduring strength of love is manifested in his final decision. He will take her back! Love is at once the most fragile and most enduring of all bonds. Though bruised and bleeding, real love lingers on.

The temptation to be vindictive has been overcome. Not many people can rise that high. The Christian response to mistreatment is difficult to come by. When Woodrow Wilson was running for reelection against Charles Evans Hughes, he was urged to answer some of the harsh charges made by Hughes. Wilson's response was, "Never murder a man who is committing suicide."[3]

Hosea not only overcame his desire to strike back, but now overcomes his wounded pride and reaches out to help Gomer who is in the process of committing moral suicide. Gomer's exciting lovers had forsaken her and the downward trend of her life had led at last to prostitution. She was the property of another. Yet Hosea says: "So I bought her for fifteen pieces of silver and a homer and a half of barley [the price of a slave]" (Hos. 3:2, The Amplified Old Testament).

It is important to note that Hosea in no way condones her actions, nor accepts her morality. Neither does he pretend that nothing has happened. This reveals the depth of his compassion. He takes her back in spite of what she has done. But his is no flighty offer: "And I said to her, You shall be [betrothed] to me for many days; you shall not play the harlot and you shall not belong to another man. So will I also be to you [until you have proved your loyalty to me and our marital relations may be resumed]" (Hos. 3:3, The Amplified Old Testament).

There must come a period of adjustment. She must give evidence of desiring to pick up the pieces. They must come to know one another again. But the important thing is that Hosea is not taking her back merely for the purpose of giving his children a mother. He is not taking her back in order to have the opportunity of punishing her by constantly referring to her past, and by refusing to touch her. What he offers is the full restoration of the marriage relationship.

THE REVELATION

We are not told what mental processes Hosea went through before offering Gomer another chance. We are not allowed to listen to his soul's argument with God's command. But we are told that God provides a theological basis for the matter. Hosea is challenged to love Gomer again, "even as the Lord loves the children of Israel, though they turn to other gods" (Hos. 3:1, The Amplified Old Testament). God is saying, "You believe in divine forgiveness, practice the same kind of forgiveness in your own life." Hosea is made aware of the fact that his own heartbreaking experience is no different from that of God's. Suddenly he sees the depth of God's love in a new dimension.

God's love is betrayed —God's love for his people has been spurned just as has Hosea's love for Gomer. Other prophets (like Amos) saw sin as the failure to live righteously. Hosea now sees it as the breaking of a covenant of love. God is more than holy, He is loving. When His love is betrayed, His heart is broken. He cares!

Hosea's tragedy magnifies God's love, His willingness to forgive. Hosea becomes the interpreter of God's love. Having been given such a tender insight, he shares it with others. Those who know him listen. He becomes the living reality of the theme he preaches.

With new vision he sees Israel as a false lover who promises faithfulness but becomes promiscuous (Hos. 2:6-12). The betrayal of Gomer is no more than what Israel continues to commit.

R. W. Livingstone observes that men have always selected gods who would patronize their actions. Dionysus became the god of the Greek who wished to be drunk. The thief selected Hermes as his god. The vicious preferred Aphrodite Pandemos.[4] Modern man is no different. He picks his gods and his heroes on the basis of his own moral level. When the demands of a moral and holy God no longer fit a man's chosen life-style, he joins himself to groups who reject such a God. The whole hippie movement bears evidence to this truth. While advocating love and peace, they make it quite clear that theirs is not the kind of moral, responsible love found in Christ, nor the peace that comes from facing up to life's problems in a responsible way. Their love is the changing, flighty love of a spoiled child, devoid of commitment, and their peace is that of a hermit who hides from life, resigns from the human race, and lives only for himself.

So, Hosea sees that his countrymen have chosen other gods, other pursuits, other values. Man has a way of staging one production after another, giving all the lead roles to someone other than God.

The wages too are the same. Sin always destroys. Gomer rebelled against her commitment and found a freedom that produced degradation and slavery. Israel was following a collision course with divine judgment that would end in the disintegration of the nation at the hands of Assyria: "They have sown the wind, and they shall reap the whirlwind" (Hos. 8:7).

God's love offers forgiveness —At last we see the emergence of good from the rubble of evil. God's message of hope is given new dimension by the agony of Hosea. Out of his grief came an awareness of hope. It was a hope for himself and for others in the grip of evil, a hope nurtured in his own frustrations. As he was able to go on loving his erring wife, so he saw God continuing to love Israel.

Hosea forgave Gomer not because she deserved it, but in spite of the fact that she didn't deserve it. He was able to forgive when he saw that God had forgiven him though he had not deserved it.

God tells us something about Himself when He suggests that Gomer be given another chance. Christ offered both the adulterous woman (John 8:1-11) and the self-righteous Nicodemus (John 3:1-21) another chance. Indeed, He offered everyone He met a new chance. This is the hope of the gospel: "He hath not dealt with us after our sins; nor rewarded us according to our iniquities" (Ps. 103:10).

God's love is not for the few who suppose they deserve it. To the self-righteous Jesus says: "I am not come to call the righteous, but sinners to repentance" (Matt. 9:13). In the presence of the intellectually proud, he says: "I thank thee, O Father, Lord of heaven and earth, because thou hast hid these things from the wise and the prudent, and hast revealed them unto babes" (Matt. 11:25).

How deeply we are indebted to the message of hope growing out of Hosea's suffering. There can be change, for anyone. No sin is too big to be mastered by God's love, if the heart desires it. The Lord's promise remains: "In the place where it was said unto them, Ye are not my people, there it shall be said unto them, ye are the sons of the living God" (Hos. 1:10). This means that God can take the same people and the same circumstances which once produced emptiness, and reverse the outcome.

Hosea's revelation of God's forgiving love stands as a rainbow amidst the storm, assuring us of hope. But keep in mind the agony which brought the revelation. There must have been many sunny, carefree days in the life of Hosea. Yet his deepest insights came when his world was crumbling. Most often this is the case. Israel learned more of God during the dangerous flight from Egypt, the frightening experience at Sinai, and the lonely wilderness wanderings than during the prosperous days of Solomon. The church has the same testimony. Those at ease in Zion have never been known for spiritual depth.

The prophets had said little of God's love. The people knew little of God's love. Then came Hosea. Those who saw and heard him learned much about God. If God wanted Hosea to love again a faithless wife, then God must Himself care about the unfaithful.

Perhaps Hosea for the first time saw himself as a rebel, a weak sinner in need of the same forgiveness needed by Gomer. When Louis XIV of France died his funeral was held in the massive cathedral of Notre Dame. Those present included the nobility from around the world. All preparations were carried out lavishly and with great pomp. The dead king was attired in the richest robes and surrounded by the accoutrements of greatness. The preacher ascended the pulpit for what everyone supposed would be a magnificent eulogy. Instead he shocked his listeners with four short words: "Only God is great."[5] Another statement of equal importance could have been made by Hosea: "Only God is good." This means we all stand amidst evil, needing His help.

Hosea's portrayal of God's love in action stood as the

supreme picture of God's concern for us all until the Savior came to bring the final word.

Suffering, whether mental or physical, is often the vehicle by which we gain new insights. But pain in itself teaches nothing. As Buttrick reminds us, pain has the power to lead only to death. If we are to be benefited by our pain, there must be the presence of a catalyst. The divine symbol of that catalyst is the cross. Two small children, upon seeing a cross in a strange church, called it a "plus sign."[6] It is indeed that. Pain coupled to life's circumstances by means of this plus sign brings cleansing and hope. The cross, the greatest symbol of suffering, is at the same time the greatest symbol of hope. It is our second chance.

Our suffering may reveal to us certain dimensions of God that before had remained hidden to us. It may be that we will someday give living form to God's forgiving love, just as did Hosea. Or it may be that our suffering will highlight some other aspect of God's dealing with men. One thing is certain. Suffering has often helped men to know God.

NOTES

1. *Pulpit Digest* (November 1970), p. 40.
2. *Pulpit Digest* (October 1970), pp. 57-58.
3. *Pulpit Digest* (October 1968), p. 60.
4. F. C. Hoggarth, "The Sceptic's Salute," *Christian Century*, XLV (1928), 1196, quoted by *Interpreter's Bible*, George Buttrick, ed., VI, p. 689.
5. Lynn Harold Hough, *The Christian Criticism of Life* (New York: Abingdon-Cokesbury Press, 1941), pp. 184-85.
6. George Buttrick, *God, Pain, and Evil* (Nashville: Abingdon Press, 1966) p. 175.

9

Suffering That Teaches Reverence for Life

"And the Lord God formed man of the dust of the ground, and breathed into his nostrils the breath of life; and man became a living soul" (Gen. 2:7).

I struggled in mental agony to find something to say at the funeral. A handsome young man lay dead by a bullet from the gun of an enraged husband who found him with his wife. Life has a way of getting so tangled when we live apart from God.

I thought about other difficult funerals. The task of saying something meaningful about life in the presence of tragedy is not an easy one. Whether or not I can voice my feelings at the funeral service, I feel that I personally must find something to say to myself, from the Christian stance.

I recall a grinding automobile crash that took the life of a young person. She was intoxicated. The search for some possible use the heavenly Father can make of such catastrophes has led me to the theme of this chapter. Sometimes evil and suffering can be used to teach us reverence for life. If life has meaning, and I am persuaded that it does, then suffering and death, which are such encompassing aspects of life, must also have meaning. These twin specters have a message for us.

George Gershwin became famous for his joyous jazz music. His song "Swanee," sung by Al Jolson, rocketed him to fame. This was followed by an international hit, "Rhapsody in Blue." One success followed another until he was awarded the Pulitzer Prize for his music in "Of

Thee I Sing." He had become rich and famous by virtue of his happy music.

Otto Kahn, speaking at a party given in Gershwin's honor, said there was one element missing from Gershwin's music—the note of sorrow. He said, "The long drip of human tears, my dear George . . . they fertilize the deepest roots of art."

Gershwin could not escape those words. He searched until he found a play about the love of a crippled Negro beggar for a girl named Bess. Neglecting work on other contracts worth thousands of dollars, he produced the American opera "Porgy and Bess," a legacy of sorrow now known the world over.[1]

If no life is complete until it has met pain, then pain must have something to teach us about life. Henry David Thoreau once said: "A man is rich (free) in proportion to the number of things he can afford to let alone." Suffering has a way of showing us that many things we feel are necessary for life are really not. Life has a meaning of its own, a reverence of its own.

REVERENCE FOR LIFE AS A TRUST

Since Genesis is the book of beginnings, we look to it to discover the beginning of suffering. And we find it. The human story begins with the creation of Adam. Standing amidst His creation of animal life, God takes earth's dust and creates human life. Adam receives the gift of meaningful life. He is made in the image of God.

As I reflect on the young man murdered by a jealous husband, I see the youthful form stilled by death and hear a message from the screaming silence: "Life is not a toy!" Toys are made to be played with, broken, and thrown away. Life is to be lived out as a trust, treated as a divine gift, viewed with reverence. Here was a young man who toyed with life, and all who walked away from his funeral that day were crushed with the realization of it. Life is not a blank check which we fill in to suit ourselves. The account is in God's name.

Samson, the strong man of the Old Testament, threw

life away because he treated it as a careless childhood game instead of a serious battle to be waged. His passion for wine and beautiful women, for following every lure of lust, led him to slavery, blindness, and death. What a waste he made of life.

Jacob, the patriarch who spent so much of his life plotting and scheming, deceiving and being deceived, said toward the end of his long life: "The days of the years of my pilgrimage are an hundred and thirty years: few and evil have the days of my life been" (Gen. 47:9). So many things remind us of the brevity of opportunity afforded by life, and sometimes tragedies and mistakes give us a deeper reverence for this thing called life.

REVERENCE FOR LIFE AS A RESPONSIBILITY

In the creation of man, one important aspect must be noted. Adam is made in God's image; he is not made a god. Adam can have companionship with the Creator, but always in the role of the created. Life is both a gift and a stewardship.

To help Adam keep this relationship in mind, God lays out certain guidelines. Adam is placed in Eden, given the responsibility of keeping it, and the obligation of obedience: "And the Lord God planted a garden eastward in Eden; and there he put the man whom he had formed" (Gen. 2:8). Some simple principles are here laid down: neither life nor property are our possessions.

If life is misused, the trust betrayed, a forfeiture results. Man's domain ends where God's begins. The tree of the knowledge of good and evil was off limits: "For in the day that thou eatest thereof thou shalt surely die" (Gen. 2:17).

Satan's temptation has to do with stepping out of the human-divine relationship, of entering God's domain as an equal: "Ye shall not surely die: for God doth know that in the day ye eat thereof, then your eyes shall be opened, and ye shall be as gods, knowing good and evil" (Gen. 3:4-5). The idea of knowing good and evil undoubtedly has to do with being able to set up your own standards of right and wrong, apart from divine rules. Try everything and decide for yourself. Make your own code.

God's pronouncement of death as sin's accompanying curse underlines the fact that life carries responsibility toward God. Death, together with the suffering that often precedes it, is a solemn reminder that life is a stewardship given by God. The psalmist, recognizing the brevity of even a long life, prays, "So teach us to number our days that we may apply our hearts unto wisdom" (Ps. 90:12).

If we feel that few people are concerned with using responsibly the days given by God, we need to be reminded that the number would no doubt be much fewer were it not for the devastation wrought all about us by the power of evil. This wreckage tells us what can be expected when life is perverted.

Genesis tells us we are not in control. We are not god of the garden. When Adam misuses his freedom, when responsibility turns into rebellion, God casts him out of Eden (Gen. 3:23-24). The message is clear and ominous. But men still disregard it. At this point, suffering becomes a megaphone by which God is able to get man's attention.

Every reader will no doubt know of someone whose life has been salvaged in the aftermath of tragedy. The prophet Isaiah tells us that he discovered God, and life's purpose, only after the death of Uzziah, a close relative and king of Israel: "In the year that king Uzziah died I saw also the Lord" (Isa. 6:1). Uzziah had ruined a good reign by spiritual rebellion. He died an outcast in a leper colony. Yet the painful aspects of his death brought Isaiah a vision of his life's purpose. He saw that he had been living selfishly and irresponsibly. A member of the royal court, Isaiah had assumed that life's meaning was dependent on a king. He came to see life had a deep meaning on its own, and that such meaning comes because of the divine dimension.

Some people never discover that life has meaning in itself. Viktor Frankl, the Christian psychiatrist who spent several years as a prisoner in a German concentration camp, tells of his own discovery of this important truth. As he and his other comrades faced the probability of death, he observed a difference in attitudes.

The question on his comrades' lips was: "Will we survive the camp?" Unless there were to be survival, they felt their suffering would be meaningless. Frankl's question was: "Has all this suffering a meaning?" Unless there were meaning to the suffering, there could ultimately be no meaning to survival. Frankl reasoned that a life whose meaning was totally dependent on the happenstance of survival could not ultimately be worth living anyway. Whether or not one escaped should not be the difference between meaning and nonmeaning.[2] It was in this context that he discovered that the real question of life is not: "What can I expect of life?" But rather: "What does life expect of me?" Frankl discovered that there is one human freedom which cannot be snatched away—the freedom to choose one's attitude in any given predicament. And so in the presence of death he found a reverence for life.

Frankl gives the case history of a mother who came to his clinic after a suicide attempt. The mother had just lost an eleven-year-old son. She was left alone with one other, older son, who was a cripple who could not care for himself. Rebelling against her fate, she tried to commit suicide along with the crippled son, but the cripple was able to stop her because, strangely enough, he did not want to die. He liked living, even as a cripple. Life still had meaning for him.

The mother was placed in group therapy. Primarily for this mother's benefit, Frankl asked another woman in the group (thirty years of age) to imagine she was eighty, and lying on her deathbed. With such a picture in mind, the woman was asked to look back on life and pretend it had been void of children but full of financial success and social prestige, then to give the thoughts that came to mind. The actual tape recording is as follows:

> Oh, I married a millionaire; I had an easy life full of wealth; and I lived it up! I flirted with men, I teased them! But now, I am eighty; I have no children of my own. Looking back as an old woman, I cannot see what all that was for; actually, I must say, my life was a failure.[3]

Frankl then invited the mother of the handicapped son to visualize herself in the same situation and look back on life. Here are her words:

> I wished to have children and this wish has been granted to me; one boy died, the other, however, the crippled one, would have been sent to an institution if I had not taken over his care. Though he is crippled and helpless, he is after all my boy. And so I have made a fuller life possible for him; I have made a better human being out of my son. As for myself, I can look back peacefully on my life; and I can say my life was full of meaning, and I have tried hard to fulfill it; I have done my best—I have done the best for my son. My life was no failure![4]

The breakthrough had come. The mother discovered meaning and reverence for life, even in her sufferings. Adam is cast out of Eden, thrust into a world of danger and death in the hope that this pilgrimage will lead him to see life as it should be seen—a gift of responsibility.

REVERENCE FOR LIFE AS A PROMISE

In this brief sojourn we find a foretaste of what life can someday be. There are enough moments of meaning to tell us that such potential good is not to be terminated by death. The fleeting glimpse of Eden stands as a promise that shall some day return fuller and richer.

Earthly life is a gift, not something we deserve. And if

life as intended by God is ever to materialize, it too must come as a gift. Without God, dust is both our source and our destiny (Gen. 3:19). But we are not left without God. Just as death stands in the way of our earthly dreams, so hell stands between us and eternal life. Looking at it another way, life is highlighted by the dark specter of death. We only see life's glory as we see it in contrast to death's shadow. And so death enhances our vision. Even so, we place the proper value on heaven, eternal life, only as we see it in contrast to hell, our just desert. It is God who delivers us from what we deserve, and points us to life, marking the route by pain and grief, beginning at the cross and leading toward eternity's horizon. Thus even the pain of death has about it the promise of life, and casts an aura of reverence upon our human existence.

NOTES

1. *Pulpit Digest* (June 1970), pp. 34-35.
2. Viktor E. Frankl. *Man's Search for Meaning* (New York: Washington Square Press, Inc., 1963), p. 183.
3. Ibid., pp. 184-185.
4. Ibid., p. 186.

Suffering for the Benefit of Others

"For even hereunto were ye called: because Christ also suffered for us, leaving us an example, that ye should follow his steps" (I Peter 2:21).

Viktor Frankl tells about one of his elderly patients who remained in a state of severe depression for two years following the death of his wife. At last Frankl asked the old gentleman what would have happened if he had died first, leaving the wife to survive and grieve. "She would have suffered terribly," replied the husband. "Then," said Frankl, "you have spared her this suffering; but now you have to pay for it by surviving and mourning her."[1] For the first time the elderly man saw some meaning to his suffering. It was a sacrifice for someone he loved.

Here we find the loftiest role possible for suffering. This is vicarious suffering—suffering which is not a penalty, but a gift offered. This is suffering for the sake of, or in the place of, someone else. At times, such suffering is involuntary, as in the case of the elderly gentleman just mentioned. The highest expression of this principle of suffering is found when entered voluntarily.

JOSEPH

The Old Testament story of Joseph (Gen. 37–50) portrays vicarious suffering that is thrust upon a young man. He has no choice. His jealous brothers sell him to slave traders who carry him to Egypt. There he becomes the slave of an army captain, is falsely accused, and thrown into prison. During the years that follow, he gains release and rises to a place of prominence in the pharaoh's regime.

As a powerful government official, Joseph is able to give food to his brothers who earlier betrayed him, and to grant choice land to the whole family that they might move to Egypt escaping the starvation of Palestine brought on by severe years of drought. It was in Egypt that the sons of Jacob would grow into a great nation. It was possible because of the earlier suffering of young Joseph. Imagine the lonely nights spent by the teen-age boy, the sense of estrangement and despair he must have felt, the anger which must have welled up in his heart, the desire he must have had to curse a world, and a God who would permit such an injustice. Yet years later, as he delivers his family, he can say, "Be not grieved, nor angry with yourselves, that ye sold me hither; for God did send me before you to preserve life" (Gen. 45:5). Joseph came to see that his suffering had been for the benefit of his family. God was able to use his suffering that others might be delivered from suffering.

CHRIST

It is to be expected that the most noble of all suffering finds its highest expression in the Savior. Here is suffering that is both vicarious and voluntary. In Him we see the blending of divine holiness and human pain.

Theologians who have sought to protect God from any idea of personal suffering have at the same time tried to make Him less a personality than we, His creation. In the heavenly Father all emotions are most fully and properly expressed. He loves us, He hates our sin, He suffers with us.

Those who see no purpose in suffering suppose it to be merely an obstacle blocking the path to any belief in an omnipotent God of love. To refuse to see any meaning in suffering is to refuse to think seriously about life. Some of the most meaningful moments of life are moments of pain.

God was grieved (suffered, if you please) over Adam's sin. He was saddened by Cain's act of murder. The widespread plague of human rebellion that brought His destruction of the world by a flood must have inflicted a deep wound to His heart. Do not suppose that God's foreknowledge of the future eliminates His concern over our failures. To know a loved one is going to betray you does not remove the heartbreak.

And so, because of the dire and catastrophic consequences of sin, God enters the sea of human suffering and walks through the valley of death that some escape from the human plight might be effected.

Prophecies of Isaiah —The most detailed advance notice concerning God's decision to deliver man through suffering came through the lips of Isaiah. Scholars disagree as to the most important historical events. In a recent list compiled by an august group of educators, journalists, and historians, the birth of Christ came out a poor fourth, outdistanced by events like the discovery of America by Columbus and Gutenberg's invention of movable type. The Bible, without hesitation, affirms the birth of Christ to be the center point of all history.

Using Isaiah as a mouthpiece, God tells Israel that their hope lies in one who is to come and suffer in their place. Though the theme of a suffering servant appears four times in Isaiah, the classic passage is found in Isaiah 52:13–53:12.

This coming deliverer is pictured in terms of his inner anguish, not his outward appearance which Sallman tried to depict in his famous painting of the head of Christ. The deliverer will have a marred visage (Isa. 52:14). He will have no comeliness that men will desire, for his beauty is to be found in his pain (Isa. 53:2), and men shun pain just as they shun the truth.

Listen to the condensed biography: "He is despised and rejected of men; a man of sorrows, and acquainted with grief . . . surely he hath borne our griefs, and carried our sorrows: yet we did esteem him stricken, smitten of God, and afflicted. But he was wounded for our transgressions, he was bruised for our iniquities: the chastisement of our peace was upon him; and with his stripes we are healed" (Isa. 53:3-5).

When we question our plight and grief, we do well to remember the Savior was well "acquainted with grief." He suffered even the ordinary deprivations of life: "Foxes have holes and birds of the air have nests, but the Son of man hath no where to lay his head" (Matt. 8:20). But rather than being concerned about His lack of possessions, He chose to be consumed with the purpose for which He came into the world. He came to "make his grave with the wicked" (Isa. 53:9), that the wicked might have hope beyond the grave. There is no more significant key to the mission of the Messiah than Isaiah's statement: "And with his stripes we are healed" (Isa. 53:5).

Incidentally, the ancient rabbis saw in Isaiah 53 the promise of the Messiah. The Targum of Jonathan, the Talmud of Jerusalem, and the Talmud of Babylon all interpret Isaiah as speaking of the coming Messiah. Only since the Jewish rejection of Christ have their authors refused to see the Messiah in this prophecy.

And so Isaiah depicts the suffering of the Deliverer. It includes contempt, physical pain, mental anguish, loneliness, and death.

The affirmation of Jesus —Then in the "fullness of the times," when God's stage was set, He sent His Son into the world and we stand confronted with the mystery of the Incarnation. "God was in Christ" (II Cor. 5:19). There is no rational explanation of how God came in the flesh. Frederick Speakman uses the analogy of sunlight to help us understand the mystery. Although the sunlight is everywhere on a sunny day, you can take a magnifying glass and concentrate that light on a crumpled piece of paper and cause it to burst into flame. Though the sunshine was everywhere, it was particularly concentrated on one spot.[2]

In the Incarnation, God did not cease to be omnipresent. The heavens were not empty of His divine presence. Jesus was not all there was of God. Rather, Jesus was the fullest revelation of God that human flesh could contain. In a wondrous, inexplicable way, God allowed a part of Himself to take on human flesh and walk in our midst with all the weaknesses known to us, and all the power common with God. As a man, Jesus prayed to the heavenly Father. Yet He affirmed, "I and my Father are one" (John 10:30).

The affirmation of Jesus concerning His mission is simple, He came "to give his life a ransom for many" (Mark 10:45). He came to suffer for the benefit of others.

In Jesus we find the kind of love that such suffering requires. Being human, He was capable of selfish ambition, but refused to yield to it. He lived among great sinners without being one. He had both the greatest reason and the greatest opportunity for revenge, but refused to take advantage of either. He was criticized on every hand, was called a glutton and winebibber, was accused of being in league with Satan, of being a blasphemer, and of playing the hypocrite. Yet He made no threats and refused to answer in kind.

He neither pouted, nor chided, nor locked Himself away from the cruel world. There was much wrong in the temple, but He did not forsake it. There was immorality abounding in society, but He did not separate Himself from humanity. While His enemies plotted His death, He wept in compassion over their city.

Being certain of the Father's will, He refused to be sidetracked by temptations or laughed out of town by the mockers. In Wasserman's musical play, a take-off on Don Quixote, the knight prepares to do battle, only to find himself faced with a knight whose chain-mail tunic has tiny mirrors mounted on it. He is the Knight of Mirrors. His shield is a polished steel mirror. The Knight's attendants have similar mirrors, and as the battle begins, Don Quixote is surrounded by mirrors so that he sees only himself. His protagonist taunts him, challenges him to see himself as the aging fool he is, as a clown dressed in a masquerade. Don Quixote is beaten to the floor by the scorn and mocking of his foes.[3]

Jesus suffered no such illusion. He lived with the truth, and chose to die for the truth, at the hands of falsehood. He had settled this matter at the outset of His ministry, when tempted in the desert by Satan (Matt. 4). It was the temptation to capitalize on one's opportunities rather than live out one's divine purpose. Victor Hugo portrays his character, Jean Valjean, facing a similar decision. Valjean was an escaped criminal who had built for himself a new and respectable life. Suddenly his world was shaken by the news that an old man in a nearby town was being tried for a crime actually committed years before by Valjean. The struggle was deep. At last he stated the alternatives: "To remain in paradise and there become a demon! To re-enter hell and there become an angel!"[4] He chose the latter, confessing his guilt to save an old man. Of course Jesus had no guilt, but His decision did involve a willingness to suffer.

The final vicarious act —There could be no simple home remedy for sin. The curse pronounced upon it in Eden remains. Death, physical and spiritual, stems from it like a malignancy. Man cannot forgive himself, nor cure himself. The divine decree remains, "The soul that sinneth, it shall die." The same divine law that tells us what is pleasing to God also defines transgressions of which we are all guilty.

Horace's ancient rules of dramatic art include one that says a god should never be introduced to the plot unless it becomes so involved that only a god can untangle it. Such is the case with regard to man's plight. Only the entrance of God can solve man's dilemma. This is what the gospel is all about. God (in Christ) offers Himself as a ransom. God (in Christ) takes upon Himself sin's curse. He dies for guilty man, that man may be pardoned. God cannot annul the curse on sin apart from paying the price—death. "Christ hath redeemed us from the curse of the law, being made a curse for us"

(Gal. 3:13). Christ absorbed in His own body the poison of our curse.

Man is unable to free himself from this curse, however he may try. An analogy might be drawn from the life of Sir Walter Raleigh. He was imprisoned in the Tower of London in 1603 by James the First and was sentenced to death. The execution was delayed year after year, and in 1616 Raleigh convinced James the First that gold could be found in Guiana. Raleigh was released to make the journey, still living under the penalty of death. The whole episode was filled with miscalculations and ended, at last, in utter failure. Raleigh returned to face the sentence of execution that had been hanging over his head for fifteen years. Death could be postponed no longer. In a real sense, every man's pilgrimage is lived out under the threat of death. Into such a milieu comes Christ. He lifts the curse by standing in our place, and dying for us.

Dickens, in his *Tale of Two Cities,* tells the story of a young nobleman, Charles Darnay, who was imprisoned during the violence of the French Revolution. Condemned to the guillotine, he faced certain death. At the last moment, a man named Carton, because he admired Darnay's wife, visited the cell, drugged Darnay, exchanged clothing with him and went to the guillotine in his place. In effect, this is what Christ did for us. And when it happened, there were no trumpets, no fanfare, no headlines to glorify His action. The only attention drawn to His death was that which came from above as the sun was darkened and the earth made to tremble.

And so suffering lies at the heart of God's redemptive plan. Leslie Weatherhead describes the cross eloquently:

> So the Cross, planned by hearts that hated, remains the strongest means of ending hate the world has ever seen; made by evil, it delivers from evil; made in fear, it saves from fear. The Cross was made by man, and, like a bandit's dagger, it was made to kill; but in God's hands it is as a sharp surgical knife, which, more than

any other instrument, has been used to cut out hate and pride and selfishness from the heart of humanity.

Surely, that is God's way again and again. The Kingdom of God has repeatedly been furthered by means which belong to the kingdom of evil. God doesn't move behind the clouds only: He uses the clouds too. Only so is He the Vindicator.[5]

The call to suffer —This same Christ who suffered for us calls us to suffer. The Scripture says of Him: "Though he were a Son, yet learned he obedience by the things which he suffered" (Heb. 5:8). He challenges: "If any man will come after me, let him deny himself, and take up his cross, and follow me" (Matt. 16:24). He openly admits this to be a call to suffer, but adds a warning to those who see no place in life for pain and self-denial: "For whosoever will lose his life for my sake shall find it" (Matt. 16:25).

At no point in our "Playboy" world is the clash between Jesus and the Hugh Hefner philosophy more distinct. Hefner rejects any philosophy that holds a man must deny himself for others. The Playboy outlook says a man should love himself preeminently and pursue only his own pleasure. Hefner says, "Get all you can." Jesus says, "Give all you can."[6] Dietrich Bonhoeffer, who was executed in a Nazi prison camp, wrote: "When Jesus calls a man, He bids him come and die." Self-denial and pain are a part of life, and a part of the calling of Him who suffered for us on the cross.

THE HUMAN ARENA

None of us can duplicate Christ's suffering. His was unique. Yet we may be called upon to share that general type of pain. We may be asked to suffer for the benefit of someone else. Self-denial for the benefit of God's kingdom is also for the benefit of other men. The poor widow who gave all the money she had, while Jesus watched in the background, was possessed of the spirit of sacrifice.

Many a parent has suffered in one way or another for the benefit of his children. The incurably ill have allowed themselves to be the objects of experimentation, to accept additional pain in the hope a cure can be found for others who are yet unborn.

I have seen wives of alcoholics go through unbearable anguish in the hope that their selfless love can salvage their loved ones' lives, and restore a home for their children.

I have seen deacons absorb the poison of criticism which otherwise would have destroyed their pastor, because they, like Stephen (Acts 6–7), saw such self-sacrifice as a calling.

Every missionary who has labored under difficult circumstances when he could have had an easier life at home has suffered that others might find Christ. Jesus warns us that we cannot "play it safe" and follow Him. We cannot find peace by avoiding the cross. We cannot live meaningfully without living painfully. "Greater love hath no man than this, that a man lay down his life for his friends" (John 15:13). The fact is that love is expensive. The cross testifies to this truth.

James Stewart says that if we treat the gospel as a kind of medicine which we take for our own benefit, to relax us and give us peace, to make us secure against all that is disagreeable, we have missed Christ's intention altogether. We are comforted by God in order that we may in turn share that comfort with others. This places a new illumination on the mystery of suffering. Can it not be that at least a part of suffering is designed to initiate us into the secret of God's comfort that we might, by means of our difficult experiences, become God's agents of help to others? In God's divine scheme, suffering has a way of being transformed into love. In the words of Thornton Wilder: "In Love's service only the wounded soldiers can serve."[7]

Buttrick says that the church's greatest failure is that

"it does not offer its own pain to God for His redemptive use, and does not deliberately seek out and share the world's pain for the same deep purpose."[8]

God's entrance into the vale of suffering, through Christ's vicarious death, adds a dimension and hope to all forms of despair. I stood recently beside the open grave of a young mother and saw the pain of loss written on the face of her husband who sought to cradle in his arms the two small children. She had been delivered from all suffering; he was left in the midst of it. Yet the time will come when neither will suffer because Christ suffered.

Christ points the way to the highest and noblest of suffering—vicarious suffering. It is highest and noblest because it originates from love. This discussion began with the instance of a husband's realization that his grieving for his dead wife delivered her from ever having to grieve for him. Only love can cause such grief, and only love can understand it to be vicarious. In a real sense, then, the highest reason for suffering can only be brought about by love, the deepest of all emotions. To love is, sooner or later, to suffer. S. R. Lysaght wrote:

> If love should count you worthy, and should deign
> One day to seek your door and be your guest,
> Pause! ere you draw the bolt and bid him rest,
> If in your old content you would remain.
> For not alone he enters; in his train
> Are angels of the mists, the lonely quest,
> Dreams of the unfulfilled and unpossessed.
> And sorrow and Life's immemorial pain.
> He wakes desires you never may forget,
> He shows you stars you never saw before.
> He makes you share with him, for evermore
> The burden of the world's divine regret.
> How wise you were to open not! and yet,
> How poor if you should turn him from the door.[9]

As we make our way through the thorn-studded paths of life, there is one who bids us follow Him: "For hereunto were ye called: because Christ also suffered for us, leaving us an example, that ye should follow his steps" (I Peter 2:21). The word translated "example" literally means "that which is written above." It referred to the large letters, or copy head, written on the pupil's paper by the teacher, under which the pupil himself was to copy the same letters in order to learn to write. In much the same fashion, we, like small children, learn to act like a Christian in every experience by looking at Christ, and trying to live as He lived.

Jesus was the perfect embodiment of a man who was true to the Father's will, and His was the fullest suffering. We need not be surprised to find that when our faith is deepest and life truest, our pain is sharpest. As we glimpse again the Son of God dying on the cross, and hear again His cry, "My God, my God, why hast thou forsaken me?" we come to understand that there will be no easy answers to the problem of suffering.

George Macdonald writes: "The Son of God suffered unto the death, not that men might not suffer, but that their sufferings might be like His."[10]

Pain is often the way to hope. David Lockard, missionary to Southern Rhodesia, writes of the death of a little girl named Gela. Though she had accepted Christ as Savior, her father was an unbelieving savage. Not knowing how the father would take the death of his daughter, Lockard waited until after the funeral and then spoke tenderly to him about God. Gela's father, with tears in his dark eyes, said, "My little girl used to run errands for me; she was always bringing me things. But today she brought me the greatest gift of all—God!"

And so we must live in the hope that somewhere along life's road, we too, perhaps by our pain, may give someone the gift of God, and thus of life.

NOTES

1. Victor E. Frankl, *Man's Search for Meaning* (New York: Washington Square Press, Inc., 1963), pp. 178-79.

2. Frederick B. Speakman, *God and Jack Wilson* (Westwood, NJ: Fleming H. Revell Co., 1965), p. 27.

3. Dale Wasserman, *Man of La Mancha* (New York: Random House, Inc., 1966), pp. 69-70.

4. Victor Hugo, *Les Miserables* (New York: Random House, Inc.), p. 198.

5. Leslie D. Weatherhead, *Thinking Aloud in War-Time* (New York: Abingdon Press, 1940), p. 105.

6. William S. Banowsky, *It's a Playboy World* (Old Tappan, NJ: Fleming H. Revell Co., 1969), p. 122.

7. James S. Stewart, *The Wind of the Spirit* (Nashville: Abingdon Press, 1968), pp. 154-55.

8. George Buttrick, *God, Pain, and Evil,* Nashville: Abingdon Press, 1966), p. 194.

9. T. Cecil Myers, *Thunder on the Mountain* (New York: Abingdon Press, 1963), p. 176.

10. *Unspoken Sermons. First Series,* Quoted in C. S. Lewis, *The Problem of Pain* (New York: Macmillan Publishing Co., 1944), p. 7.

11

Suffering Without Reason

"Behold, I cry out, Violence! But I am not heard; I cry aloud for help, but there is no justice" (Job 19:7, The Amplified Old Testament).

I drove the car methodically, insulated from the outside world by the steady drone of the motor and troubled thoughts of my heart. The death notice had come to us a complete surprise. The funeral was marked by the usual shock and numbness felt by all families when death has left a vacant chair. Now we were returning home. At last the long silence was shattered abruptly by my wife's stark words: "You have been preaching on the reasons for suffering; why do you think Janie died?"

The question itself was no shock for it had pursued my thoughts from the moment we had learned of the death. Janie had been very close to us. I had performed her marriage ceremony. I had rejoiced to see her and her husband growing in their Christian experiences through the brief years that followed. Now at the age of twenty-six she was gone, leaving behind a grief-stricken husband and two bewildered children. In a matter of days a chronic condition had become complicated, then fatal.

My answer was not very helpful. Trying to verbalize the thoughts which had been coursing through my mind, I said, "I don't know why Janie died. God alone knows that, and only time (or eternity) will reveal His answer. She died as a casualty in the war against death, a war that sooner or later fells everyone. The use God will be able to make of her death remains to be seen. Perhaps her passing will teach some of us a deeper reverence for life as a gift. It could be the means of spiritual growth for those close to her. If her death leads to the conversion of those in her family who are not Christians, she will have suffered vicariously. We could go on with our speculation, but for the moment, the truth is that the reason for her sudden death is mysterious. It lies beyond our understanding." My wife said no more, not because I had answered her question, but because I had confessed there was no human answer. Of one thing I was certain, there are no experts on suffering.

This painful experience has led me to a reexamination of Job's suffering. We know that God allowed Job to suffer to reveal the reality of his faith, to show there are men who serve God out of reverence rather than out of a selfish desire for personal gain. Yet we know this only by the divine revelation of Scripture. Job never did know why he suffered. The whole ordeal remained a mystery to him. Perhaps nowhere else will we find so helpful a study of someone beset by suffering for which he can find no reason.

THE FRUSTRATIONS OF MYSTERIOUS SUFFERING

Each of us searches for simple, clear-cut reasons for the things which befall us. There is something deeply aggravating about the inexplicable. As previously indicated, Job was not patient in our sense of the word. A better translation speaks of the "endurance of Job." If we look carefully at that endurance we find it marked by frustration, impatience, and even anger. He does not curse God, but he makes it quite clear that he is not at all happy with God and quite openly curses the day of his birth: "After this opened Job his mouth and cursed his day. . . . Let the day perish wherein I was born, and the night in which it was said, There is a man-child conceived. . . . [Why] died I not from the womb?" (Job 3:1-3, 11).

While Job did not curse God, he came dangerously close to it. He makes no bones about blaming God for his heartache, and casts considerable doubt upon the justice of a God who could stand by and let such tragedies happen to a man who has lived right: "Behold, I cry out, Violence! But I am not heard; I cry aloud for help, but there is no justice. He has walled up my way, so that I cannot pass. . . . He has stripped me of my glory . . . my hope has He pulled up like a tree. . . . He counts me as one of His adversaries" (Job 19:7-11, Amplified Old Testament).

In bitterness, Job sums up life by saying, "Man that is born of a woman is of few days, and full of trouble" (Job 14:1). Job finds himself in the predicament of believing in a God who permits the unbelievable, of loving a God whom he feels like hating. Interspersed with his cynical remonstrances are gleams of his faith that still survives: "Though he slay me, yet will I trust in him" (Job 13:15). "I know that my redeemer liveth, and that he shall stand at the latter day upon the earth: and though after my skin worms destroy this body, yet in my flesh shall I see God" (Job 19:25-26).

Although these outbursts of faith bespeak a hope beyond this earthly life, we must be honest enough to notice that Job's chief reason for verbalizing such hope is to affirm that the day will come when everyone will know his innocence, and his mistreatment. Lest his arguments be forgotten, he yearns for them to be immortalized: "Oh that my words were now written! oh that they were printed in a book! That they were graven with an iron pen and lead in the rock forever!" (Job 19:23-24). Job is a little like a woman who asked me once if all deeds would be made known on the Day of Judgment. Though she was not personally prepared for that eternal examination, she rejoiced in it because, as she put it, "Everyone will know how mean my husband has been to me."

Job cannot seem to escape self-pity as he looks about and observes that the wicked live long lives, have many children, no tragedies, prolific herds, much money, many holidays, easy deaths, and in the whole process tell God to get lost, and make it stick (Job 21:7-15).

Although Job's comments are a part of his conversation with three so-called friends who are certain some secret sin is at the root of Job's suffering, we recognize that Job is indirectly scolding God through these remarks, like an angry wife who directs harsh retorts at a child for the benefit of the listening husband. Sooner or later, the indirect challenge must confront God. And it does.

THE DIVINE DEBATE

Job's physical suffering is not to be minimized, but it is secondary to his philosophical agony. His neat world with its simple answers has become a complex, mixed-up storm of confusion. Like a man fighting for his life in a hurricane, Job struggles to maintain his faith, and his life-long belief in the justice of God.

At last, in the midst of his storm, God speaks: "Then the Lord answered Job out of the whirlwind, and said, Who is this that darkeneth counsel by words without knowledge?" (Job 38:1-2).

In a moment, the setting is reversed. God is no longer absent or silent. The mortal who has been spreading the word around to the effect that he wants to put some questions to God, if he can find Him, has suddenly been found by Him. But it is God who asks the questions: "Gird up now thy loins like a man; for I will demand of thee, and answer thou me" (Job 38:3). Moments before, Job was searching for God. Now we have the feeling he would like to escape God.

A matter of perspective —God's questions are designed to bring out the qualifications of the mortal who has been so vocal in his criticism of divine providence. The questions are basic: Where were you when I created the world? What holds up the world? Who put the stars in place and set the bound of the sea? Do you understand light? Do you understand darkness? Have you looked beyond the doorway of death? Do you understand the natural elements that produce hail and snow? Do you perceive the power that keeps the heavenly bodies on course? Are the secrets of lightning known by you? Do you understand the cycle of life in the animal world and the instincts that guide these creatures? (Job 38:4—39:30).

God's questions are designed to help Job place himself in proper perspective. If Job has no understanding of the secrets of the natural world, why should he demand to know the secrets of the supernatural world?

The desired effect comes. Job recognizes how foolish he has been to propose to understand all that happens: "Then Job answered the Lord, and said, Behold, I am vile; what shall I answer thee? I will lay mine hand upon my mouth. . . . I will proceed no further" (Job 40:3-5).

Job finds himself in the same predicament as the children who were trying to put together a puzzle of the world. Being unschooled in geography, they were having great difficulty. Then they noticed that on the backside of the puzzle was the picture of a man. Here was something they understood. They were then able to fit the pieces together.[1]

Leslie Weatherhead tells of a little ant he saw crawling along the pulpit cushion one Sunday. Upon arriving at the gap in the cushions, the little ant seemed confused. It hesitated. First it went one way and then the other. There seemed to be no route to follow. Perhaps its wife was home waiting lunch. What a major problem was posed by a crack in the cushions! The little ant did not realize it was in a church, had never heard of London, the city in which its tiny existence was located, knew nothing of the world, let alone the vast spaces of the universe or the problems confronting man. All it could see was a chasm that halted its journey.[2]

It was this kind of perspective God wanted Job to have—to see his mortality and his ignorance of most all the basic concepts of the world about him. Why should Job expect to be informed on matters of divine purpose when even the mundane world about him remained a mystery?

A matter of trust —The debate has its desired effect. Job lays his hand on his mouth, determined to ask no more questions. No longer does he seek an opportunity to instruct God. He realizes that it is he, and not God, who is unaware of life's total picture.

In humility he trusts God: "Then Job answered the Lord, and said, I know that thou canst do every thing, and that no thought can be withholden from thee. . . . I have uttered that I understood not; things too wonderful for me, which I knew not" (Job 42:1-3).

Job discovers that he can trust God's purposes. No longer does he suspect that the world is a team of runaway horses who caught God by surprise. Up to now, Job has been certain he could do a better job of managing the universe than God has done. Now, after seeing his total ignorance, he is willing to let God remain the head man. Somehow, Job is no longer obsessed with having his day in court in order to prove himself to be an innocent sufferer. He comes to see that the spirit of his relationship to God is more important than the letter. His outward conformation to God's law has hidden an inner attitude of rebellion: "Wherefore I abhor myself, and repent in dust and ashes" (Job 42:6).

ACCEPTANCE OF THE MYSTERIOUS

Job has been told no divine secrets. His knowledge of the reason for his suffering is still at an impasse. No new facts have been added. Yet his attitude has been changed. He recognizes that he is to be allowed no nearer the truth than he was at the beginning of his quest: "The Lord gave, and the Lord hath taken away; blessed be the name of the Lord" (Job 1:21).

He has not received an answer, but rather the strength to withdraw the question. A transformation has taken place. The question has been replaced by faith. Since he is not God, he must be content with being man, and must learn to live with the limited understanding of which man is possessed. His new view of God's greatness enables him to accept life by accepting God: "I have heard of thee by the hearing of the ear: but now mine eye seeth thee" (Job 42:5). No longer will Job depend on philosophical hearsay. He has stood in God's presence, or rather, he has discovered God standing with him in his misery, and somehow that makes everything different. He sees God where before he saw only his trouble. He cannot understand the latter, but he can trust the former. In the words of P. T. Forsyth, God's gift is not "an answer to a riddle but a victory in battle. . . . We do not see the answer; we trust the answerer. . . . We do not gain the victory; we are united with the Victor."[3]

Gerald Kennedy gives the account of a young Jewish girl who managed to escape a ghetto in Warsaw by climbing over a wall and hiding in a cave. Before death found her, she scratched on the cave's wall three things: "I believe in the sun, even when it is not shining; I believe in love, even when feeling it not; I believe in God, even when he is silent."[4] As Fosdick reminds us, Jesus did not say, "I have explained the world," but, "I have overcome the world" (John 16:33).[5]

And so I am left with the original question, "Why did Janie die? I still have no answer. Someday I will have, perhaps in this world, more likely in the world to come. I remember another tragedy that occurred while I was a student in the seminary. A foreign missionary to Africa, Wimpy Harper, drowned. Just months before, he had spoken in our chapel. He and his family had gone to Nigeria in 1950. A man of great strength and dedication, he soon became a leader in his mission area. Because of this he had been selected as one of three missionaries to open a new field in East Africa. It was to this new area that he returned shortly after my hearing him in 1958.

Just months after Harper's return, three new missionary couples arrived in East Africa and to celebrate the event a picnic on the beach was planned. They found a beautiful spot along the beach of gleaming white sands and soon most of the party were swimming in the lazy blue green waters of the Indian ocean, unaware of the dangerous undertow that lurked under the surface and rushed down the coral reefs and out to the great expanse of sea. Suddenly the swimmers were in its grip. In the frightening nightmare that followed, those on the beach and others in the shallow water were able to rescue everyone except Harper. They watched, horrified and exhausted, as he was swept out to sea. With every ounce of strength he tried to return to the land to which he had come eight years before. But it was not to be. He was gone.

I remember the shock when the news of his tragic death was announced in the chapel where he had such a short time before spoken. I remember my Missions professor reading a letter from Harper's wife a few weeks after her return to America. In it she confessed her lack of any answer as to why her husband died, yet she affirmed that prayers were being answered and that God's presence was real.

Seven years later, Jesse Fletcher stood looking down on the same beach and blue green water. He was writing a book about the life of Wimpy Harper and had come to gather material.[6] He tells how deceptively innocent the beach looked and how remote seemed the trade winds that produced the deadly undertow. As he was swept up with his inner questions of the "why" of Harper's death, Fletcher's reverie was broken by the voice of one of the missionaries. It was Arville Senter, and he said, "Wimpy died here, and the story of his death was the instrument God used to lead Pauline and me into missionary service. We're here because of what happened down there seven years ago." Another missionary, Betty Bedenbaugh, added, "There are nearly a dozen of us here because of Wimpy's influence."[7]

I remember the day that Professor Cal Guy faced the seminary student body with the news of Wimpy's death and challenged them to consider the call of missions.

Scores responded and went out to the corners of the earth.

Wimpy's death has not been explained, but with the passing of the years, additional good continues to grow out of that deep loss. The full answer must wait for eternity, but even now a part of it is emerging where once there was only mystery. From the stance of faith we affirm that "behind the dim unknown, Standeth God within the shadow, keeping watch above his own."[8]

Suffering is the one common denominator. We are all in it together. I look at some instance of suffering and say it could have been for any one of many reasons. It could be playing any of the roles assigned to it in these pages, or all of them. They may be mixed and interlaced. The one thing I am sure of is that all suffering has purpose when God is allowed to stand in its midst. Like it or not, life is filled with the mysterious. If we do not understand why good things happen to us, we should not be too perturbed about our inability to explain the evil that comes our way. Perhaps we should join Christopher Morley in defending the presence of the mysterious. He writes:

> I went to the theatre
> With the author of the successful play.
> > He insisted
> On explaining everything; he told me
> What to watch, the details of direction,
> The errors of the property man,
> The foibles of the star.
> He anticipated all my surprises and spoiled the evening.
> Never again! But mark you
> The greatest Author of them all made no such mistake.[9]

We need to remember that the greatest mysteries of all await us in eternity when we view the new heaven and the new earth prepared for those who in this life walk by faith.

NOTES

1. *Pulpit Digest* (May 1970), p. 52.
2. Leslie Weatherhead, *Salute to a Sufferer* (New York: Abingdon Press, 1962), pp. 54-55.
3. P. T. Forsyth, *The Justification of God* (London: Independent Press, 1948), pp. 208-212, 220, 221, quoted in the *Interpreter's Bible,* ed. George Buttrick, (Nashville: Abingdon Press), Vol. III, p. 1197.
4. *Pulpit Digest* (December 1970), p. 56.
5. *Interpreter's Bible,* Vol. VI, p. 570.
6. The book is *Wimpy Harper of Africa* (Nashville: Broadman Press, 1967). Jesse Fletcher is personnel secretary of the Foreign Mission Board of the Southern Baptist Convention.
7. Ibid., p. 141.
8. James Russell Lowell, "The Present Crisis" in *Masterpieces of Religious Verse,* ed. James Dalton Morrison (New York: Harper and Row, Publishers, 1948), pp. 522-24.
9. Christopher Morley, "No Coaching," in *Questing Spirit,* eds. Halford E. Luccock and Frances Bretano (New York: Coward-McCann, Inc., 1947), p. 418.

Part Four

POWER FOR SUFFERING

12

The Heavenly Father's Love: Love That Lasts

"Beloved, let us love one another: for love is of God; and every one that loveth is born of God, and knoweth God. He that loveth not knoweth not God; for God is love. In this was manifested the love of God toward us, because that God sent his only begotten Son into the world, that we might live through him. Herein is love, not that we loved God, but that he loved us, and sent his Son to be the propitiation for our sins. Beloved, if God so loved us, we ought also to love one another. No man hath seen God at any time. If we love one another, God dwelleth in us, and his love is perfected in us. Hereby know we that we dwell in him, and he in us because he hath given us of his Spirit. And we have seen and do testify that the Father sent the Son to be the Saviour of the world. Whosoever shall confess that Jesus is the Son of God, God dwelleth in him, and he in God. And we have known and believed the love that God hath to us. God is love; and he that dwelleth in love dwelleth in God, and God in him. Herein is our love made perfect, that we may have boldness in the day of judgment; because as he is, so are we in this world. There is no fear in love; but perfect love casteth out fear: because fear hath torment. He that feareth is not made perfect in love. We love him, because he first loved us. If a man say, I love God, and hateth his brother, he is a liar: for he that loveth not his brother whom he hath seen, how can he love God whom he hath not seen?" (I John 4:7-20).

When we think of love, we usually think of romantic love. Every wedding ceremony involves two people, each of whom pledges love for the other "until death do [them] part." Yet in any given year, there are one-third as many divorces as marriages. This is a tragic reminder that some love does not last.

One cannot help but be struck by the depth of the love illustrated by the Irish poet, Thomas Moore. While Moore was away from England on an overseas trip, his exceptionally beautiful wife, a former actress, contracted the dread disease of small pox which left her lovely face marked with scars. She was so certain that her husband would be repelled by her ugliness that she was afraid to write and tell him what had happened. Informed by a mutual friend, Moore composed a poem especially for his wife in an effort to assure her that his love was not dependent upon her continued beauty:

Believe me, if all those endearing young charms
   Which I gaze on so fondly today,
Were to change by tomorrow and fleet in my arms,
   Like fairy-gifts fading away,
Thou wouldst still be adored, as this moment thou art,
   Let thy loveliness fade as it will . . .
And around the dear ruin each wish of my heart,
   Would entwine itself verdantly still.[1]

Yet, though we are touched by the depth of love exhibited by Moore, we recognize that it exists only marginally. At the center of genuine love stands God, the source of everlasting love.

THE ORIGIN OF LOVE THAT LASTS
(I John 4:7-8)

Love that lasts must of necessity have something distinctive about it. In the Greek world there were three basic types of love. There was a kind of brotherly love (phileo) which was often used to speak of the warm love one had for his close friends and family.

Then there was the *eros* type of love, the classical expression of which is found in Plato's *Symposium* where he describes it as a primitive type of love much akin to the sexual desire and marked by passionate craving, not only for physical beauty, but for beauty that included that of the mind and the soul. Basically this kind of love is thought of as romantic love based on physical attraction.

Inspired by the Holy Spirit, the New Testament writers selected a word for love, *agape,* which is only sparsely found in non-Biblical Greek literature. When it is found, it usually has meanings such as "to be content with," "to like," "to esteem," "to prefer." It was this rather plain and colorless word that the translators of the Old Testament used when speaking of the love of God to man and, in turn, man's response to that divine love. Thus the heavenly Father chose to select a relatively unused and untainted word to describe His love, and then to fill that word with new and unique meaning so that it became distinctly Christian.[2]

This *agape* love came to be identified with the Spirit of self-sacrifice whereby the good of others is sought, regardless of the cost involved. It came to be the kind of love that was marked by totally unselfish giving, regardless of the worth of the recipient. This is indeed the only kind of love that can last because if one's love is constantly based on the merit of the person loved, the very depravity of human nature will sooner or later cause that kind of love to cease. If love is based on selfish desires and goals, then that love is doomed to failure. If the goals are reached, there is no further need for the love. If the goal becomes unreachable, there is still no further need for that kind of love. Either way it is doomed to failure.

This background for the meaning of God's kind of love is necessary if we are to understand all that is involved in the statement: "God is love" (I John 4:8, 16). Science has often characterized God as nothing more than cosmic energy or scientific law. Moralism has often depicted God as nothing more than a kind of moral oughtness. The Greek philosophers often saw God in terms of pure mind or wisdom.

In the New Testament, God is spoken of as "Spirit" (John 4:24) to help us understand that His unseen presence makes Him constantly available to each of us. He is described as light (I John 1:5) because He illuminates life in its proper perspective. The writer of Hebrews (Heb. 12:29) describes Him as a consuming fire (cf. Deut. 4:24) to dramatically underscore His attitude toward sin. However, the highest statement about God to be found in the New Testament is: "God is love." The Gnostics conceded that God was spirit and light, but the idea that God was love was totally foreign to them.

Keeping in mind that *agape* is noted for its self-sacrifice and total giving, we understand that to say "God is love" is to say that everything God does is marked by sacrificial, total giving, without regard to personal cost, or to the recipients' merit. Therefore the statement "God is love" does not reveal merely one more attribute of God, but rather reminds us that every attribute of God, every activity of God, is rooted in His love.

THE SUPREME ILLUSTRATION OF A LOVE THAT LASTS
(I John 4:9-10)

It is to be noted that the only place in the New Testament that states that "God is love" (I John 4:8, 16) sets forth the greatest illustration of God's love in terms of the Incarnation: "For God is love. In this was manifested the love of God toward us, because that God sent his only begotten Son into the world, that we might live through him. Herein is love, not that we loved God, but that he loved us, and sent his Son to be the propitiation for our sins" (I John 4:9-10).

Here is the finest description of *agape* love. It involves the kind of total giving that involved God taking upon Himself human flesh and dying on a cross to pay for the sins which we have committed in direct rebellion against Him.

We can lay no claim to this kind of love having originated with us: "Herein is love, not that we loved God, but that he loved us, and sent his Son." When the Son became clothed in flesh and walked among us, He found us spiritually dead and naturally rebellious. He found a world directed by hate and envy rather than love of one another.

If God's every activity issues out of love, then we have but to note His many activities to understand all that is involved in His kind of love when it is put into action. It is God's love that led Him to enlighten the understanding of men that He might thereby expose sin for what it really is. It is because of His love that He can be pictured as a consuming fire that will not tolerate the continued activity and presence of sin, since sin always ruins. God would not go to such great pains to defeat sin if it were not that He cares about what happens to us.

Contrary to popular belief, God's love does not rule out the possibility of His wrath. God's wrath and utter opposition to sin has been announced ahead of time. His love has led Him to allow His Son to be crucified that we might not have to pay the penalty for our sins. But to turn from His Son, His ultimate expression of love and care, is to choose to remain with our sin that will destroy us. Therefore we read: "He that believeth on the Son hath everlasting life: and he that believeth not the Son shall not see life; but the wrath of God abideth on him" (John 3:36). God must maintain wrath toward sin if He is to be a God who cares. And unless God cares, He cannot possibly have love.

Just as a parent hates evil in his child, and a wise ruler hates evil in his own society and seeks to oppose it, so God's love leads Him to have wrath toward sin. The more a parent loves his child, the more determined he will be to correct the evil tendency that seeks to lead him astray. If necessary, such a parent will ardently punish his child in an effort to separate him from his evil inclinations. All of this is done out of love. The parent who doesn't care will spend no time in seeking to correct his child. If the child is ever to grow up, he must be rewarded for right, and punished for wrong. It is for his best interest. Even if it should become evident that the child is not going to respond to such loving care, the parent must continue it in the interest of the other children in his family. So God, even when the sinner is beyond hope of ever amending his ways, must, for the sake of the universe, punish sin. This is God's righteousness acting out of love. Law says: "Righteousness is love in the imperative mood."[3] God must act in utter consistency if He is to be righteous. Again Law says that "Duty is the consistency of love to its higher end." Genuine love carries with it certain responsibilities toward consistency, whether we speak of God's love for us, or of our love for God.

Perhaps the most important aspect of God's love is that it is active. He pursues us. With Him, our destiny is a matter of serious intent. While He allows us a choice, He is not a disinterested bystander.

C. S. Lewis, perhaps the most gifted Christian writer of our century, tells of God's pursuit by depicting God first as a master angler playing his fish, then as a determined hunter. Suddenly everything Lewis read turned his thoughts to God. Hear him describe God's active search of love so like the experience of Frances Thompson in his "Hound of Heaven:" "The fox had been dislodged from the Hegelian Wood and was now running in the open . . . bedraggled and weary, hounds barely a field behind."[4] Like an invincible chess player, God began to make His final moves. Looking back, Lewis observes that all over the board his own pieces were in the most disadvantageous positions. When at last the moment of conversion came, Lewis was alone in his room, a kicking, struggling, resentful prodigal who found himself the victim of God's love—but a soon-to-be happy victim who described his conversion in terms of being "Surprised by Joy."

THE MATURITY OF LOVE THAT LASTS
(I John 4:12, 17-18, 20)

Although we usually think of love as being an intangible emotion, there is a sense in which we can mark the progress that love makes in us. John speaks of this as he says, "His love is perfected in us" (I John 4:12). The word *perfected* carries with it the idea of purpose being accomplished. God's kind of love makes progress —it grows within us. It is going somewhere. His love has never really accomplished His purpose for it until it has begun to reproduce in our lives that same kind of sacrificial love.

God's love is in terms of a tremendous investment that led to the crucifixion of His own Son. The expression "the love that God hath to us" is better translated "the love which God hath *in* us." This sets forth Christians as those in whom God has invested His love.[5] This investment should bear fruit by working a change in every Christian's heart.

Love others—John reminds us that there is one way we can be certain whether or not God dwells in us— whether or not our Christianity is real. The test is simple: "If we love one another, God dwelleth in us, and his love is perfected in us." If one's faith surrender has been genuine so that God's kind of love has been allowed into the heart, the passing of time will see a marked progress in one's ability to love others. This is something you have to learn to do. There is a Christian art of caring.

Simon Peter once found himself led to the house of a Gentile, a man named Cornelius, whereupon he beheld those of that household genuinely converted. To accept them was to go across the grain of everything he had been taught concerning the hated Gentiles. However, because God's love had lodged in his heart, he recognized that he must either accept these as brothers in Christ, or engage in personal battle with the Living God (Acts 11:17). It was a difficult lesson, but Simon Peter had to begin to learn to love.

We need again to remember the basic definition of God's kind of love. It has to do with giving, without regard to the cost, keeping foremost the welfare of the recipient, and remembering that such love cannot be withdrawn merely because the recipient does not deserve it.

John sets forth a very simple, but fearful test: "If a man say, I love God, and hateth his brother, he is a liar: for he that loveth not his brother whom he hath seen, how can he love God whom he hath not seen?" (I John 4:20). Calvin says: "It is a false boast when anyone says that he loves God but neglects his image which is before his eyes."[6] Stott says this is like the person who claims to be intimate with a foreigner, but cannot even speak his language, to claim as parents those with whom there is no resemblance.[7]

John reminds us that it is easier to love if our love has some tangible object. Therefore, it should be easier to love our brother, since we can see him, than it is to love a God whom we cannot see. It is difficult to test anyone's love for the unseen God, but it is rather simple to know how much he is able to love his brother.

Few things tell you more about a man than how much he is able to love others. Plutarch once wrote concerning love and said that it seemed to be one of the secrets of Christian morality. He noted that the keynote of Christian love was never in terms of self-protection, but rather that of self-giving in an effort to help others. Plutarch noted that this was directly opposite to the outlook of the Stoic who always emphasized the self, and explored every means possible of protecting the self from all emotions or outward problems that would disturb inner tranquility. On the other hand, Christians stressed the welfare of others and their personality and forgot the claims for themselves. William Sloan Coffin, Jr. has said: "Man is not what he eats, not as he thinks, man is as he loves."[8]

Another interesting point is raised by John as a further incentive toward loving one another. It is found in the opening words of the same verse that contains the command to love one another: "No man hath seen God at any time. If we love one another, God dwelleth in us, and His love is perfected in us." This raises the question of how men who are not believers are to be aware of God—how they are to see God. Certain pagan religions led men to believe that they could see God through mystic rites and dramas. The Christian maintains that men are able to see God in Jesus Christ, but also that in a secondary way men should be able to see God by the way Christians love one another. Love in itself is one of the greatest possible witnesses a Christian can have. It is at this point that even the highest kind of pagan love that might exist within families and relationships utterly fails. Christian love, if it is genuine, always finds a way to manifest itself in such fashion that God is glorified, and to that extent revealed.

An American journalist serving in China watched while a Catholic sister cleansed the gangrenous wounds of hospitalized soldiers. The journalist said to her: "I wouldn't do that for a million dollars." Without pausing, the sister replied: "Neither would I."[9] It was her way of saying that only love could lead to such self-giving—God's kind of love.

Overcomes fear—Once again John uses the idea of love making permanent and purposeful progress within: "Herein is our love made perfect, that we may have boldness in the day of judgment . . . there is no fear in love; but perfect love casteth out fear: because fear hath torment. He that feareth is not made perfect in love" (I John 4:17-18). "Fear" is accompanied with a definite article which, in the Greek language, means that a specific kind of fear is in question. The remainder of the verse explains the particular fear with which John is dealing—it is the fear of the judgment. As love matures, if it is God's kind of love, it will gradually cast out all fear of the final day when we shall stand before

133

Him. Every man should have reverent respect and awe for the heavenly Father. However, God does not intend that His children should live in terror. It is the kind of fear which is marked by terror that John is concerned with at this point. This kind of fear robs man and leaves him less than human. This is the kind of fear that evil despots use in brainwashing in an attempt to dehumanize and paralyze the persons involved—to destroy their personality and free will. This is the kind of fear John depicts in relationship to the spirit of anti-Christ. Left to themselves, men know much of this kind of fear. Archeologists working with the records of the ancient Hittite empire have found the book of prayers belonging to Myrsilis the Second who ruled from 1336 to 1304 B.C. One of these prayers read: "From my heart drive out the pain, O God, from my mind lift the fear."[10]

Writing in the *Expositor's Bible,* Alexander MacLaren states that there are four possible conditions of the human soul with regard to love and fear: "Without either fear or love; with fear, without love; with fear and love; with love, without fear."[11]

John tells us that "perfect love casteth out fear." There is a simple reason for this. Keep in mind that God's kind of love is marked by an utter disregard for self, by total giving for the welfare of others. On the other hand, fear is self-centered. It is concerned only with personal welfare. It is aroused by any threat to one's own self. To eliminate fear, one must cease to be completely obsessed with his own welfare. Only love can do this. When one is rid of "unhealthy self-consciousness" one is rid of fear. Love organizes personality around God and man. This is indeed a higher plane. It is utter, self-giving love to God that in turn exhibits itself in the same kind of love for man and no longer fears the judgment.[12] Everything is now in God's hand, and the complete love for one's brother leaves no agonizing worries about being called to account on that matter. Everything has been committed in trust to God.

Therefore, love will not keep house along with bitterness, selfishness, hatred, or fear. All must go, and the degree to which one casts out these evil roommates is indeed an accurate measure of one's love. One can accept life's trials only if he has learned to love.

Paul Scherer tells of a young boy terrified by the coming of the doctor who laid out his shining instruments. The lad had begged his father not to allow the doctor to come. Not only was the doctor allowed to enter, but the boy's father held him securely while the doctor did his work. Now any adult understands that what the father did was done in love, but that young lad failed to understand it so.[13] He failed to grasp the meaning of parental love, just as we often suppose that our pains are evidence that God does not love us.

No need to fear eternity when it is viewed as merely another expression of God's love which He has invested in us. The only cause for fear concerning the judgment is to be found in the lives of those who have rejected God's love. A part of His love includes His desire to allow us the freedom to choose. He will respect our right of choice. Yet as long as we have life and opportunity He never ceases to love us and care about us. As long as we are interested, He never says, "I can do nothing more for you."[14] His is indeed a love that lasts, and He calls us to be like Him.

NOTES

1. *Pulpit Digest* (May 1970), p. 20.
2. C. H. Dodd, *The Johannine Epistles* (New York: Harper & Brothers, 1946), pp. 110-12.
3. Robert H. Law, *The Tests of Life* (Grand Rapids: Baker Book House, 1968 reprint), p. 87.
4. C. S. Lewis, *Surprised by Joy* (New York: Harcourt, Brace and Company, 1955), p. 225.
5. George G. Findlay, *Fellowship in the Life Eternal* (New York: Hodder and Stoughton), pp. 346-47.
6. John Stott, "The Epistles of John" in *The Tyndale Bible Commentaries* (Grand Rapids: Wm. B. Eerdmans Publishing Company, 1964), p. 171.
7. Ibid., p. 161.
8. T. Cecil Myers, *Thunder on the Mountain* (New York: Abingdon Press, 1963), p. 166.
9. George Buttrick (ed.), *The Interpreter's Bible* (New York: Abingdon Press), XII, p. 281.
10. E. M. Blaiklock, *Faith Is the Victory* (Grand Rapids: Wm. B. Eerdmans Publishing Company, 1959), p. 55.
11. Clyde Breland, *Assurance of Divine Fellowship* (Nashville: Broadman Press, 1939), p. 238.
12. *Interpreter's Bible*, p. 286.
13. *Pulpit Digest* (November 1969), p. 28.
14. Paul Tournier, *A Place for You* (New York: Harper & Row, 1968), p. 200.

13

The Presence of the Living Christ

"For if, when we were enemies, we were reconciled to God by the death of his Son, much more, being reconciled, *we shall be saved by his life*" (Rom. 5:10).

The execution had been carried out with all the brutality common to crucifixions. The body of the condemned man lay in a cold tomb. He had done nothing worthy of death, yet He was dead—as dead as if He had deserved to die.

So mused the two disciples of Jesus as they walked the dusty road from Jerusalem to Emmaus on that quiet Sunday morning. They did not believe Christ had risen though they had heard rumors that some women had found the tomb empty. When He joined them on that dusty road they were unaware of His identity until evening was upon them. As last Christ revealed Himself to them and vanished from their sight. Reflecting on the whole experience, the two said, "Did not our heart burn within us, while he talked with us by the way?" (Luke 24:32).

In that moment, those two men discovered a great truth. All other religions are just that; Christianity is companionship with the living Christ. We live in a world that will some day kill us. At times we feel that we, like Christ, are being crucified unjustly. But we look to Him who said, "If the world hate you, ye know that it hated me before it hated you" (John 15:18). The living Christ not only experienced the most severe agony possible, but He stands with us as we face suffering, and suffers again with us.

Our power for facing life's painful experiences comes from Christ. The word *comfort* literally means "strengthened by being with." In the Biblical sense, only the presence of Christ brings genuine and lasting comfort. When Paul prayed for physical healing, God's answer was not a miracle but a promise: "My grace is sufficient for thee" (II Cor. 12:9).

Although defining God's grace defies human wisdom, we do not miss the mark far by viewing the presence of Christ as the grace God bestows upon us. Christ's presence on the cross was God's grace in action, and His daily presence in our lives is a continuation of God's grace. This means that peace and comfort is not dependent on the absence of all tears and conflicts, but rather on the presence of Christ. His promise still stands: "I will not leave you comfortless: I will come unto you" (John 14:18).

This is not to say that He appears to us visibly or overwhelms us with His presence. The heavenly Father revealed Himself to us in Jesus Christ. The Bible, divinely inspired, tells us of this Christ, of His death and resurrection. The Holy Spirit, God's unseen presence, is in a sense the presence of the living Christ. As we open ourselves to His unseen presence, we grow in our realization that we are not alone in this universe.

PRESENT IN THE FACE OF EVIL

No one who looks seriously on life can escape the awareness of evil's magnitude. The satanic infiltrates every aspect of life. We find ourselves as frustrated as the kindly old man who purged his garden of thistles only to see that they had invaded his neighbor's garden. Feeling an obligation to do something about such a state of affairs, he laboriously weeded his neighbor's garden. Looking up from his task he was gripped with despair as his eyes fell on a whole hillside covered with thistles. He had to face a bitter truth. He could never cleanse the world of thistles. What was even worse, when he arrived at church the next Sunday he saw that the altar flowers were Scotch thistles. Even his church had been invaded.[1] And sooner or later, if we are honest, we see that evil is not merely all around us, but indeed is within us.

Our own efforts to defeat evil are always piecemeal and ineffective. The story of man's attempt to create utopias is the story of failure. The whole problem of pollution is an illustration of man's failure to face up to the radical nature of any cure.

Joseph Wood Krutch tells of an ordinance passed in Pima County, Arizona, (where he lived the last years of his life) to deal with air pollution. The ordinance made one exception. The copper smelting plants were exempted because they were an important part of the economy. The problem was that these copper plants were responsible for something like 90 percent of the air pollution.[2]

The problem of evil is the problem of spiritual pollution. Only radical measures can avail. In answer to our human predicament, God came in Jesus Christ and paid the price of death that laid on our heads. He was crucified for our sins! Christ took our guilt upon Himself. The innocent suffered for the guilty. The guilt that would have condemned us was removed—if we will only commit ourselves in faith to this Christ. The Bible explains: "For if, when we were enemies, we were reconciled to God by the death of his Son, much more, being reconciled, we shall be saved by his life" (Rom. 5:10).

Two very important matters are dealt with in this little verse. First, the death of Christ made possible our reconciliation to God. Sin's payment, which is death (both physical and spiritual death) has been paid. This payment accrues to our account as we repent and follow Christ.

Now notice the second aspect of this verse. Though it was Christ's death that opened to us the way to forgiveness and eternal life, it is His life, His living presence, that delivers us day by day from despair and defeat.

Read it again: "Much more, being reconciled, we shall be *saved by his life.*" God does not pardon us and straightway desert us. We are not given the name of Christian and then left to face life in our own strength. The living Christ walks with us daily to help us overcome temptations and to strengthen us when we walk in sorrow's vale. God's salvation is not merely future. It involves the present also. He will not permit our life to be without meaning and purpose.

A newly converted alcoholic still has a tormenting craving to battle. He must have the presence of the living Christ each day if he is to overcome his demonic thirst. In much the same fashion, we each face demonic forces as sin continues to wreak havoc all about us. We draw our daily strength from Him who never forsakes us. We know His love is real for it led Him to the cross. We know His power is real for He overcame the power of the grave. He lives, and because of this, we too can live. Life can go on for us whatever we have to face.

The aged apostle John declared: "Truly our fellowship is with the Father, and with his Son Jesus Christ" (I John 1:3). The word "fellowship" is the Greek word *koinoia.* Its original setting was the business world. When men went into a business partnership where the fortune of each was bound up with the venture, the word they used to describe the partnership was *koinonia.* The Holy Spirit chose to take this word and use it to describe our relationship with Christ. Our destinies are joined together. All our hopes are wrapped up in this venture of faith. He is our partner in life. He shares our joys and our sorrows. We face life with Him.

Yet it is important that we understand that He does not exempt us from life's rough edges. Weatherhead reminds us that God's power needs to be understood in terms of the "ability to achieve purpose." There is such a thing as power that defeats purpose. This kind of power is weakness. Weatherhead uses the illustration of a hockey game. Suppose a huge giant of a man observed his first hockey game and was told that the point of the struggle was to put the ball into the net at the end of the field. Picture the confusion that would result if the huge giant dashed on the field, knocked players left and right, ran over the referees, clubbed the goal-keeper, and deposited the ball in the net. This would be power, but all purpose would have been defeated. If such behavior continued, the whole game of hockey would be destroyed.

It would have required greater power on the part of the giant to have exerted restraint. So God's power is often evident in restraint. Suppose a father observes his small sons trying to build a tower out of toy blocks according to a description he has given them. They quarrel. Again and again the partially built tower is toppled by the careless efforts of the sons. The father has several options. He can run the boys out of the nursery and do the job himself. He can stand by and prevent every miscue so that the tower never topples. He can make spineless slaves of the boys by beating them so that they cease quarreling and perform like robots. Or, he can watch them quarrel, make mistakes, or topple the tower, and yet restrain himself in patience, being content to try to show the brothers how to get along and build, until at last they have accomplished the task. The first three options would appear to be power in action, but would defeat the purpose. The last action requires restraint, and patience, and allows the possibility that when the boys complete the tower they will assume they have done it all by themselves. Yet only the last alternative allows them to learn to live as brothers, and to accomplish anything in the process.[3] So Christ does not step in to do our work, read our lines, or take our blows. But He stays beside us all the while and gives us strength to go on.

PRESENT IN THE STORMS

Although Christ does not abolish the storms, He is with us in the storms. This means we must realize that faith does not still the raging winds, but rather trusts God in their midst.

On one occasion, Jesus rebuked His disciples because of their panic when the small boat in which they were riding was caught up in a sudden and violent storm. Literally, Jesus called them "little-faiths" (Matt. 8:26). They had not come to feel that His presence with them was enough. They still did not understand that there is no defeat for those who walk with Christ. Even if the ship sinks, or the tumor is malignant, or the crash is fatal, we are with Him who holds the universe together, in whose hand is all of life and eternity.

PRESENT IN OUR GETHSEMANES

Theodore Wedel lays his finger on a part of our problem when he observes that the only gospel many ever hear is the *Reader's Digest* version depicting the log-cabin-to-the-White-House success story as being the norm.[4] When life doesn't turn out this way for us, we do well to remember that the Incarnation was a White-House-to-log-cabin experience, ending on a cross.

We are ever confronted with the danger of hearing without really hearing, of seeing without really seeing, and of living without really living. Unless we learn to see Christ in every scene, we will be as confused about reality as the man in the ancient Oriental legend who discovered the first mirror but did not know what it was. After a while, he decided it was a portrait of his father. He placed it in his private shrine at home and noticed that with the passing of time, the portrait looked more and more like his beloved father. By chance, his wife discovered the mirror one day and declared, "Just as I suspected, another woman, and not a very pretty one at that."[5]

Our Gethsemanes will come. They may not occur in a garden, as did our Lord's, but they will be marked by the same loneliness and soul searching. On that last night before His crucifixion, He prayed for us (John 17:20). He prayed that we might be able to live in the midst of evil without partaking of it. He prayed that Satan would never have our interests and influence (John 17:15-17).

He asked that all of us who believe in Him might be unified with one another, and with Him (John 17:21). And then He prayed that we might some day be with Him and behold His glory (John 17:25). He was concerned about us, and still is concerned about us. I find strength knowing this.

Some of our Gethsemanes will grow out of the dark shadows of death's valley. After the initial shock at the death of someone dear, a bereaved person often struggles with deep depression and loneliness. The words of Jesus on the cross seem all too fitting: "My God, my God, why hast thou forsaken me?"

Often there follows feelings of guilt. You cannot help but remember offenses committed against the loved one, or you feel somehow you are to blame for the death, either directly or indirectly. Words spoken in anger return to haunt the conscience. In such times it is good to know that the Christ who made forgiveness possible is beside us to grant continuing forgiveness so that sorrow can be a time also of confession and healing.

It is quite possible for us to be rather selfish in our grief. This accounts for the fact that although we be assured that our dead loved one is with the Lord, we may still grieve beyond what is normal or healthy. Kierkegaard, in his treatise *The Sickness unto Death*, maintains that we are all victims of despair, whether consciously or unconsciously, and that any means of coping with this despair, unless through religion, is either satanic or unsuccessful. Kierkegaard says that our despair, in the last analysis, is not over the object of our loss, but actually over ourselves. The despair over a lost sweetheart is actually despair over the self-without-the-sweetheart rather than over the sweetheart. Being with the sweetheart allowed an escape for the self. With the sweetheart gone, the self has no such escape and must stand alone. This principle applies to any loss, be it status, money, or whatever. What we cannot bear is the thought of self denuded from the other object.[6] What a relief to know that the presence of the living Christ means that we are never left just to ourselves.

Albert Camus, in *The Plague,* pictures the lonely frustration that marks our times. In his novel a North African city is besieged by an epidemic of bubonic plague. Following the initial wave of panic, the populace, like soldiers the night before a great battle, give full sway to their animal lusts. Camus sees the whole world, because of the Bomb, as a battlefront. All meaning and all hope are gone. There is no future, no reason to go on. If man is indeed alone, then Camus is right. But the presence of the living Christ adds a new dimension to our existence. The despair about us does not drive us to Satan, but to Christ. We hear the Bible say, "[Cast] all your care upon him, for he careth for you" (I Peter 5:7).

We hear again this timeless promise, "And, lo, I am with you alway, even unto the end of the world" (Matt. 28:20). His presence is constant. He is the eternal God. Though walking in human flesh, He said, "Before Abraham was, I am" (John 8:58).

When the aged apostle John was exiled on the prison isle of Patmos, the risen Lord appeared to him and said, "Fear not; I am the first and the last: I am he that liveth, and was dead; and, behold, I am alive for evermore, Amen; and have the keys of hell and of death" (Rev. 1:17-18).

The living Christ, our Lord, has run the full gamut of human experiences and grief. He knows our problems and frailties. His presence led the apostle Paul to affirm: "I am persuaded, that neither death, nor life, nor angels, nor principalities, nor powers, nor things present, nor things to come, nor height, nor depth, nor any other creature, shall be able to separate us from the love of God, which is in Christ Jesus our Lord" (Rom. 8:38-39).

When taken as a prisoner to Rome to stand trial, Paul wrote of the experience as follows: "At my first answer no man stood with me, but all men forsook me. . . .

Notwithstanding the Lord stood with me, and strengthened me" (II Tim. 4:16-17).

Yes, it is His presence, and not the absence of conflict, that brings peace. During the Nazi bombing of London that began in 1939 many English children were evacuated from dangerous areas. Amazingly, it was found that these children suffered greater emotional upset from being separated from their parents than they had suffered from being exposed to physical danger. As long as we know Christ is with us, we can face life's pains. Chad Walsh says it beautifully:

> I have called to God and heard no answer,
> I have seen the thick curtain drop, and sunlight die;
> My voice has echoed back, a foolish voice,
> The prayer restored intact to its silly source.
> I have walked in darkness, he hung in it.
> In all my mines of night, he was there first;
> In whatever dead tunnel I am lost, he finds me.
> My God, my God, why hast thou forsaken me?
> From this perfect darkness a voice says, I have not.[7]

NOTES

1. George Buttrick, *God, Pain, and Evil* (Nashville: Abingdon, 1966), p. 44.
2. *Pulpit Digest* (December 1970), p. 58.
3. Leslie Weatherhead, *Salute to a Sufferer* (New York: Abingdon Press, 1962), pp. 48-51.
4. *Pulpit Digest* (December 1970), p. 10.
5. Ibid., pp. 33-34.
6. William Barrett, *Irrational Man* (New York: Doubleday & Co., Inc., 1958), pp. 150-51.
7. Chad Walsh, *The Psalm of Christ,* (Philadelphia: The Westminster Press), Copyright 1963 by W. L. Jenkins.

14

The Certainty of Divine Providence: What Do We Need to Fear?

"If God be for us, who can be against us?" (Rom. 8:31).

A distinguished author being interviewed on television stated in no uncertain terms his disbelief in God. His explanation was that he could not possibly believe in a God who played hide-and-seek with men, never revealing Himself.

While the Christian does not claim to have seen God, he does affirm an awareness of God's presence and a belief that God is actively at work in the world. With Shakespeare we conclude: "There's a Divinity that shapes our ends, Rough hew them how we will."

Divine providence is a term used to express the Christian belief that God is at work bringing about His purposes, and that nothing can defeat this divine process. Jesus Himself asserted: "My Father worketh hitherto, and I work" (John 5:17). God's rest from His creative labors in no wise indicates His withdrawal from the activity of His creation. Not only does He hold the universe together with His power (Col. 1:17), but He will see to it that this universe fulfills His designed purpose in creation.

To carry out His plans, God will go to any length. No person or thing is unimportant to Him. The Koran tells an interesting story of how Gabriel was sent by God to do two things on earth. First, he was to prevent King Solomon from sinning by forgetting his prayer hour amidst his exultation over his royal steeds. Second, Gabriel was to help a little yellow ant on the slope of Ararat which was about to perish for want of food and shelter. Gabriel saw one task just as important as the other since any command of God is important, and since all matters are important to God. While the Koran is not a part of our Scripture, the point is well taken for the Bible affirms God's interest in every person and every detail. Jesus promised His disciples that not even a sparrow fell to the ground unnoticed by God, that even the hairs of their heads were numbered (Matt. 10:29-30).

The certainty of God's providence puts a new light on birth and death. T. S. Eliot, in "Little Gidding," wrote:

> What we call the beginning is often the end,
> > And to make an end is to make a beginning.
> The end is where we start from.

Life is indeed more than the brief moments between birth and death. From the Christian stance, death is the beginning, "the end we start from." Just as any full biography must be written looking back from the death of the subject involved, so history, which is but the biography of the world, must be viewed from the end backward. Such a task would be impossible were it not for the revealed message of the Bible which tells us in general terms about the death of the world. The final chapter belongs to God. The victory is His.[1] Evil is to be vanquished and righteousness will prevail. God's children will be delivered and eternity will begin. This is the certainty which sustains us in the meantime as we battle amidst life's storms and tears.

AMIDST OUR GUILT

Not the least of our problems is this matter of personal guilt. Not only do we feel guilty about having mistreated loved ones now departed, but we recognize a basic guilt about our misuse of all of life. Sin is real and it has found a resting place in our hearts far too often.

The apostle Paul shares with us his own personal

struggle with sin, and the accompanying despair: "O wretched man that I am! who shall deliver me?" (Rom. 7:24). The best part of it is that he shares his discovery. He has found deliverance through faith in Jesus Christ (Rom. 7:25). Hear him:

> Now then, there is no judgment against them who are in Christ Jesus . . . because what the law could not possibly do, since it was dependent on fleshly strength, God did in sending his own Son as a man, and as a sacrifice for sin, to defeat sin personally (Rom. 8:1-3, translation mine).

We can almost hear Paul heave a sigh of relief. His spiritual experience has been as frightening as that of an alpine climber who frantically feels his rope slipping and at the height of his panic suddenly feels a solid ledge beneath his feet. The assurance that God upholds us with His hand (Ps. 37:24) is but one of the glorious aspects of divine providence.

God's determination to bring each of our lives to fullness and purpose assures us that even our failures and blemishes can be transformed. A costly handkerchief, ruined by a blot of ink, was once shown Ruskin by a friend who bemoaned the loss. Ruskin took the handkerchief and in a very skillful and artistic way made a beautiful design on it, centered around the blot of India ink. The transformed handkerchief was then returned by Ruskin, more beautiful because of the blemish. As Tennyson said, "Men may rise on stepping stones of their dead selves to higher things."[2] And so amidst our guilt, what need we fear? The only one who has the power to condemn us is the Christ who died in our place, for our guilt (Rom. 8:34). The faithful have His word that all is well. Forgiveness is complete.

AMIDST OUR LONELINESS AND ALIENATION

I have never known a person who did not at some time feel all alone. There is so much about us that strives to separate families and friends. Our age of technology tends to impersonalize relationships and people are reduced to numbers on punched cards.

To a world of displaced and lonely people, God offers a family—His family. He wants to adopt each of us as His own child, through Christ. His Spirit calls us to commitment to Christ, and when we yield to the Holy Spirit, we become sons of God: "For as many as are led by the Spirit of God, they are the sons of God" (Rom. 8:14). A new relationship and a new attitude results: "For ye have not received the spirit of bondage again to fear; but ye have received the *Spirit of adoption* [italics mine], whereby we cry, Abba, Father" (Rom. 8:15).

In other words, the old attitude of fear, fear that comes from feeling all alone, no longer binds us. Our new attitude is that of a child newly adopted by a loving father. The attitude of belonging permeates everything. If we feel the treasures of earth eluding us and the honors of men passing us by, we do not feel a sense of failure for we are "heirs of God, and joint-heirs with Christ" (Rom. 8:17a). There seems to be one stipulation. Those who inherit His glory need to be aware that to do so is to also inherit His suffering: "If so be that we suffer with him, that we may be also glorified together" (Rom. 8:17b). To walk with Him in glory we must first walk with Him in the here and now. This means a commitment that often leads away from the crowds and the glitter, that draws the world's disdain and Satan's fire.

While God is committed to watching over us, He is not overly protective because He does not want to smother our spiritual growth. I remember a young lady who since her early youth had suffered from muscular distrophy. It was not until she had reached her midtwenties that her parents had the courage to let her do things on her own. Until that time she had been utterly miserable, feeling life had no meaning. Once she began to leave the house by herself, undertake the danger of crossing streets, and find part-time employment she was a transformed person. I am sure it was not easy for the parents to see her burn herself trying to cook, to see the bruises that accompanied her efforts toward responsibility. Standing back and letting her try was probably their greatest act of love for her.

By the same token, God does not make of us puppets that He manipulates by strings. Each of us, in one way or another, is handicapped. Yet He lets us make decisions, take chances, get bruises. He refuses to be too available because each of us has a potential which cannot be reached apart from life's precarious experiences.

We must never construe God's apparent absence as a lack of love. Malachi tells us that God looks upon His children as His most precious treasure (Mal. 3:17).

A pastor in a nearby town tells of being called to the hospital by a young mother who was dying. She explained that the only time she had been to his church was for baptism after a revival in the small mission church where she attended. Her family stood quietly in the room. The husband wore old work clothes that had patches on top of patches. The children were poorly clad also. The young mother's eyes swept around the room at her family and she said, "Aren't they wonderful!" Then she paused, and for a moment saw them through the pastor's eyes, and said, "Oh, they don't look like much to you, but they mean everything to me." I have a feeling God looks upon His family in the same way.

AMIDST OUR PAIN AND FRUSTRATION

There is to be a future glory for God's children: "For I reckon that the sufferings of this present time are not worthy to be compared with the glory which shall be revealed in us" (Rom. 8:18). "Reckon" is a bookkeeping term. In the language of a certified public accountant, Paul says he has added up all the columns and the sum total of our destined glory far outweighs the sum total of our present problems.

Yet there are times when our current milieu so overwhelms us that we despair of a future glory. There are times when we question the process by which we are arriving at eternity. Humility in the presence of divine providence is not always easy. We can see too many inequities.

A physicist tells how students frequently came to him with criticisms of the present world operations, both generally and in particular. His method was to let them get it all out of their system, ask them for their suggestions as to how they would run the world, and then say to them, "My idea of hell is for you to have to live in the kind of world you seem itching to put together."[3]

We must remind ourselves that if we suddenly had the power to do anything we desired, we would not have the wisdom to use it. God promises us one thing: the triumph of His purpose. To those who have responded to His call to purpose, He promises that good can be brought out of every circumstance (Rom. 8:28). In the meantime, I am reminded that my own triumph is to be found in sharing Christ's: "Thanks be unto God, which always causeth us to triumph in Christ" (II Cor. 2:14). And so we bow to providence:

> I learn as the years roll onward
> And leave the past behind,
> That much I had counted sorrow
> But proves that God is kind.
> That many a flower I'd longed for
> Had hidden a thorn of pain,
> And many a rugged by-path
> Led to fields of ripened grain.
>
> The clouds that cover the sunshine
> They cannot banish the sun,
> And the earth shines out the bigger
> When the weary rain is done;
> We must stand in the deepest shadow
> To see its clearest light
> And often in wrong's own darkness
> Comes the living strength of light.[4]

How often God uses the thorns to accomplish His ends. George Macdonald reminds us that God will not force any door. He may send a storm to shake the house, crumble its foundation, and blow in its window, but He will not enter until invited. Macdonald says, "Every tempest is but an assault in the siege of love."[5] Many problems are solved when the love that has been locked out is allowed inside.

So much is accomplished by God's use of little things. It is said that Columbus observed a flight of pigeons to the southwest and changed his course toward the West Indies whereas had he held his course he would have landed at Virginia. Such a small incidence prevented the dominion of North America by Spain. An early winter defeated Napoleon's attempt to conquer Russia. Robert Browning wrote, "We find great things are made of little things, and little things go lessening till at last Comes God behind them."[6]

Adoniram Judson is a case in point. Greatly influenced by Jacob Eames, a brilliant student at the college in Providence, Judson turned from faith to deism until he came to consider himself an infidel. Are we to consider it an accident that he later stopped at an inn where the only vacant room was next to that of a dying man? Are we to believe it only chance that kept Judson awake that night, listening to the groaning of that young man who lay dying, and wondering about his own death? Are we to believe it merely blind fate that the following morning Judson discovered that the young man who died was none other than Jacob Eames whose rationalistic philosophy had ill prepared him for death? Judson found again his faith, not by accident, but by providence. God had intervened to reclaim his life and direct him toward the mission fields of distant Burma.

When Joseph faced his brothers who had years before sold him into slavery, whose lives and families were totally dependent on Joseph's position under Pharaoh, he wisely spoke words that have since been fitting on many other occasions: "As for you, ye thought evil against me; but God meant it unto good, to bring to pass as it is this day to save much people alive" (Gen. 50:20).

AMIDST THE THREAT OF DEATH

On one of his birthdays, Vachel Lindsay wrote that he was certain he heard the crickets chirping, "Three months till frost." Carson McCullers, in his novel *Clock Without Hands,* depicts the character named J. T. Malone as a man who has just learned he is slowly dying of leukemia. With only a few months to live, J. T. Malone looks at life as a "clock without hands." He is never certain as to just what time it is on his life schedule. Having no one with whom he feels he can talk of death, he begins attending the largest church in town. But disappointingly he finds there only a folksy message for people who are going to live, not for a man about to die.

Death is a subject we think of often, but speak of seldom. This should not be. Anything common to all men should be discussed. Though there are many separators —war, famine, persecution, deprivation (Rom. 8:35)— death is the final one.

Coleridge describes the fearsome apprehension of the ancient mariner in terms that could well be applied to man's awareness of death:

> . . . Like one that on a lonesome road
>   Doth walk in fear and dread,
> And having once turn'd round, walks on,
>   And turns no more his head;
> Because he knows a frightful fiend
>   Doth close behind him tread. . . .

The writer of Hebrews tells us Christ's death destroyed death's ultimate power over us. He came to "deliver them who through fear of death were all their lifetime subject to bondage" (Heb. 2:15). It is said that Louis XV would not allow death to be mentioned in his presence. He sought to avoid all contact with cemeteries and funerals. Can you imagine the terror brought to the heart of such a man as death slowly descended upon him? Carlyle gives a vivid description of the death of Louis XV and refers to death as the "King of Terrors." Louis XV laid down to die in the midst of an age of skepticism and atheism. Those closest to him scarcely knew whether or not to offer prayers and administer last rites according to his Catholic faith.[7]

Into such a world came Christ. He drank our death potion in order to "taste death for every man" (Heb. 2:9b). He did it "that through death he might destroy him that had the power of death, that is, the devil" (Heb. 2:14). This is a vital part of God's providence. He provides for our death. We cannot escape the experience, but we can prepare for it. We no longer have to be terrorized by it. Victor Hugo once said:

> Have courage for the great sorrows of life,
> and patience for the small ones, and when you
> have laboriously accomplished your daily task,
> go to sleep in peace, God is awake.

The psalmist said the same thing: "He that keepeth Israel shall neither slumber nor sleep" (Ps. 121:4).

We are not to identify divine providence with fate. The mood of fate is seen in the lines of Thomson:

> Every struggle brings defeat
> Because Fate holds no prize to crown success;
> That all the oracles are dumb or cheat
> Because they have no secret to express,
> That none can pierce the vast black veil uncertain
> Because there is no light beyond the curtain:
> That all is vanity and nothingness.[8]

Providence speaks of purpose. Fate speaks of despair. Providence tells us of help. Fate tells us we are helpless. The rising sales of horoscopes indicates far too many people spend time reading about their fate as fixed by the stars instead of finding God's will that leads to life.

Paul, in an effort to assure us that nothing can separate us from God's love and purpose, lists some things often supposed to do so. Among them are life (with its many disappointments), death (with its apparent finality), the unseen spiritual powers all about us, and the concluding words, "nor height nor depth" (Rom. 8:38-39). "Height" and "depth" are terms from astrology that indicate the highest and lowest points of the orbits of heavenly bodies. At its height, a star supposedly had more influence on your affairs than at its depth. Paul lays all of this aside. Nothing can frustrate God's purpose for your life.

We are not to suppose this to be a blanket affirmation for all. Part of God's purpose involves personal choice. Men can choose to live apart from divine purpose by living apart from Christ. Concerning those who thus persist in the face of knowledge, the Scriptures affirm: "For this cause God gave them up" (Rom. 1:26). But to all who respond to God's call in Christ, glory is certain (Rom. 8:30).

Do not suppose that divine providence rules out the need of prayer. Jesus prayed and admonished His disciples to do likewise. Prayer does more than affect the attitude of the one who prays. It lays hold of divine power. God is responsive to our prayers. We do well to pray "if it be thy will" as a way of recognizing God's right to ignore our request should it be contrary to His purpose. We could easily be asking for something that would do us harm. He will not give us what is not for our best interest. In the words of an unknown author:

> He prayed for strength that he might achieve:
>   he was made weak that he might obey.
> He prayed for health that he might do greater things;
>   he was given infirmity that he might do better
>   things.
> He prayed for riches that he might be happy;
>   he was given poverty that he might be wise.
> He prayed for power that he might have the praise of
>   men;
>   he was given infirmity that he might feel the need of
>   God.
> He prayed for all things that he might enjoy life;
>   he was given life that he might enjoy all things.

> He received nothing that he asked for—all that he hoped for;
> his prayer was answered—he was most blessed.[9]

Our universe is not so closed that God cannot interrupt His natural laws. The natural thing would be for God to interrupt them when necessary. As a Jewish rabbi said, remarking about the troubled state of Israel and the possibility of a way out, "One is the natural way and the other is the miraculous way. The natural way is that God will help us out of this mess. The miraculous way to try to do it by ourselves."[10]

Life is not easy, but we must not judge it too quickly. A play is not over until the last act and the final curtain. As a youth, Joseph Parker was confronted by an agnostic who asked what providence did for Stephen when he was being stoned. Parker's answer was that providence enabled the martyr to say, "Lord, lay not this sin to their charge."[11] This in itself is no small miracle.

Because we know the ending, we persevere; yes, we are even optimistic. In spite of wars and rumors of war, we know the victory belongs at last to the Prince of Peace. Shelley portrays the spirit of encouragement much akin to that given our hearts through Christ:

> And when the fight is fierce, the warfare long,
>   Steals on the ear, the distant triumph song;
> And hearts are brave and arms are strong again.

Helen Bagby Harrison, in the biographical account of her parents who were pioneer missionaries to Brazil, tells of the death of her mother. As Helen and her mother boarded a plane on their way to a family reunion, they found that the pilot was an old friend. As they settled back in their seats, Mrs. Bagby remarked, "My, but it's good to know the pilot."

Shortly after being airborne, Mrs. Bagby clutched at her heart. She was in mortal pain. Helen asked the pilot to turn back and land, which he did without hesitation. At her mother's funeral service, Helen told of the experience, of her mother's words about the pilot, and went on to say how wonderful it is to know the pilot when the soul sets out on that last journey from which no one returns.[12] "What shall we then say to these things? If God be for us, who can be against us?"

NOTES

1. See Helmut Thielicke, *I Believe* (Philadelphia: Fortress Press, 1968), pp. 202 ff.
2. Alfred Lord Tennyson, *In Memoriam,* I.
3. George Buttrick (ed.), *The Interpreter's Bible* (New York: Abingdon Press) III, pp. 118-85.
4. "The Silver Lining," *Pulpit Digest* (March 1967), p. 53.
5. *Pulpit Digest* (December 1970), p. 21.
6. A. H. Strong, *Systematic Theology* (Chicago: The Judson Press, 1907), Three Volumes in One, p. 429.
7. Thomas Carlyle, *The French Revolution* (New York: The Macmillan Co., 1925), Vol. I, see pages 16-21.
7. Thomas Carlyle, *The French Revolution* (New York: The Macmillan Co., 1925), Vol. I, see pages 16-21.
8. James Thomson, "The City of Dreadful Night," quoted in Emile Cailliet, *Journey into Light* (Grand Rapids: Zondervan Publishing House, 1968), p. 13.
9. In "Prayer Poems," compiled by O. V. and Helen Armstrong, Abingdon-Cokesbury Press, Nashville, 1942 by Whitemore & Stone.
10. *Pulpit Digest* (June 1968), p. 60.
11. *Interpreter's Bible,* IV, pp. 647-48.
12. Helen Bagby Harrison, *The Bagbys of Brazil* (Nashville: Broadman Press, 1954), p. 154.

15

The Christian View of Death

> "But of the tree of the knowledge of good and evil, thou shalt not eat of it: for in the day that thou eatest thereof thou shalt surely die" (Gen. 2:17).

> "And when Jesus had cried with a loud voice, he said, Father, into thy hands I commend my spirit: and having said thus, he gave up the ghost" (Luke 23:46).

R. Lofton Hudson speaks for many when he says that death is a four-letter word—"obscene, vulgar, nasty, not to be used on stage or in polite society."[1] Pascal spoke of our human condition in terms of a chain-gang, all of whom were condemned to death. Each day some were killed in the sight of others. Each watched and waited for his turn.[2]

Doctor Carl Jung indicates that in psychoanalysis every person over thirty-five years of age is dominated, either consciously or unconsciously, by the fear of death and the religious problem.[3] One thing we can be sure of: "We shall all die." Death is the common denominator which makes all of us have a common need. The Bible affirms: "It is appointed unto men once to die" (Heb. 9:27). Since we cannot avoid death, the question of prime importance concerns how we shall face death. As Christians, we live by faith, but how shall we face death?

FACE THE FACTS

The place of death —One of the facts we must face is that death has a place in the total scheme of things. It is a sentence that has been passed upon all humanity. Following His creation of man and woman, God warned against rebellion by saying that in the moment it came they would "surely die" (Gen. 2:17). When human rebellion passed from the realm of possibility into the realm of reality, death entered the human story and God proclaimed: "Dust thou art, and unto dust shalt thou return" (Gen. 3:19). Man's sin, then, is the source of death. In terms we can easily understand, the New Testament affirms: "The wages of sin is death" (Rom. 6:23). When man grew tired of walking beside God and decided to walk as God, he linked himself to the perishing dust of which he had been made. Whatever path he took led at last to a grave. Death is our constant reminder that we are men and not gods. Whether a man lives and dies in the same community in which he was born, or whether he sets foot on the moon, makes little difference as far as the final end is concerned. A grave waits for him. Medicine may prolong his life and doctors may perform miraculous surgery, but he will at last die. The doctor always fails, ultimately. Every patient he has will die.

Our fear —We should not find it too surprising that we fear death. Death is unnatural. It is an intruder. The Bible speaks of death as an enemy (I Cor. 15:26). Alfred Hocke, the psychiatrist, wrote in his book *Annual Rings* that it was strange indeed that man, who understands he cannot escape the law of death, has such a difficult time in accepting it. He cannot seem to bear the thought that his world is to be wiped out some day. He does not want to "collapse beside the road while the others continue, chattering as though nothing had happened."[4] The fact is that it would be very abnormal for a Christian not to have some fear of death. We should not be too worried if we find such fear in our own hearts.

Christ's defeat of death —As Christians, we believe that Christ has defeated death on our behalf: "O death, where is thy sting? O grave, where is thy victory? The sting of death is sin; and the strength of sin is the law. But thanks be to God, which giveth us the victory through our Lord Jesus Christ" (I Cor. 15:55-57). The "sting of death" refers to the horror and threat that death involves. The most fearful thing about physical death is that it is merely the outward sign of a spiritual death that is to culminate in hell. When we say that Christ has defeated death for us, we are speaking of the second death, of spiritual death. It is at this point that we have victory in Christ. Since death was pronounced upon man because of spiritual disobedience, the most dire results of it are spiritual. The second death, or spiritual death, is hell itself. Christ's death for our sins delivered us from this destiny of hell.

People who go to a doctor often ask for an honest diagnosis. If we genuinely want such a diagnosis on all of life, the Bible stands ready to give it. Where is life going? It is going toward death and hell. If you ask: "How long do I have?" the only answer that can be given is: "Perhaps just today." It is into this predicament that Christ comes. His death on the cross paid the wages of our own sin. Hell is no longer our destiny. Yet we still must die physical death. "Flesh and blood cannot inherit the kingdom of God" (I Cor. 15:50). Christ's death for our sins has delivered us from hell but not from facing physical death. It is the spiritual death from which we are delivered, and yet in that deliverance even physical death loses its horror. It is, then, this physical death which the Christian still faces.

FACE UP TO LIFE

A Christian is not prepared to face death until he has faced up to life. Thielicke describes life in terms of a long corridor down which we walk. Spaced along the corridor are doors through which we walk. The doors have knobs only on the front side. Once they have closed behind us we cannot open them and retrace our steps.[5] As we pass through each door, we leave behind a piece of time. To live is of necessity to grow old. We should neither fret about this nor ignore it. We must learn to accept life as a journey during which we grow older.

The proper attitude toward growing older is merely to live one day at a time. This is what Jesus had in mind when He said: "Take therefore no thought for the morrow: for the morrow shall take thought for the things of itself" (Matt. 6:34). Since all of life is to be considered a stewardship before God, we must learn to offer each piece of our life, each section of our earthly time to the Lord. In youth, we offer Him our strength. As we grow older, we have less strength to offer, but more poise and maturity and experience. Therefore each period of our life finds us with qualities peculiar to that period alone, which when offered to God brings a sense of satisfaction and purpose. We must learn to be grateful that we are privileged to offer not merely our youth but also our silver years to the Lord.[6]

We must learn to face up to the fact that life will contain unhappy experiences. Since every man we meet will someday die, we must learn to expect a certain amount of suffering and sickness to precede death. Since men have the freedom of choice, we must learn to expect the innocent to sometimes be the victims of the guilty. Since an eternity waits wherein final judgment will be rendered and a rectification of all things will be made, we must learn to be reconciled to the fact that in this life not everything is set straight.

We need to prepare ourselves for the fact that sooner or later we will go through the shock and depression of losing loved ones. There will be times when we have only questions, and no answers. There will be times when our faith is weak and clouds cover the sun. This is life.

FACE UP TO CHRIST

In spite of the fact that the Christian is one who has placed his faith in Jesus Christ, there come times when he must again renew his vows and remind himself of this Christ and of His words. The noted missionary E. Stanley Jones said that every man "needs re-conversion at forty on general principles!" He explained that by the time we reach the age of forty we have a tendency to settle down and lose something of our spiritual expectancy. We tend to become a product of our environment. The world comes to be "much with us." Its propaganda has taken its toll on our life. The promises of Christ have been caused to fade.[7] In other words, we must not only renew our vows to Christ, but we must remind ourselves of his promises about death. Even though we know we have been delivered from spiritual death (hell) we must remember His promises about the physical death which we still face. As I have already mentioned, it is but natural for us to have some fear of death. The reason is simple. Life was our first gift from God. Death came as an intruder. The intruder still remains with us, but life will at last triumph.

Surrender —We learn from Christ that physical death is to be looked upon as a surrender. Though we fear it, and wish to postpone it, we are not so foolish as to flee madly from it. We recognize there comes a time when we must surrender to it. We learn a great deal about death as we read the account of the death of our Savior. Listen to Him again as He says: "Father, into thy hands I commend my spirit." The Scripture then continues: "And having said thus he gave up the ghost" (Luke 23:46). Biographies of great Christians abound with this same picture of peace by looking death in the face. Johann Albrecht Bengel, a godly scholar, once said: "When a pilgrim enters that better world, the door opens and a little breath of heaven always sweeps over those most closely involved, strengthening them until their turn for the good journey arrives."[8] We sense something of this as we read of the death of Jesus Christ. One of those nearby who felt this fresh breath of life at the moment of His death, reacted as follows: "Now when the centurion saw what was done, he glorified God, saying, Surely this was a righteous man."

I remember a dear Christian mother, eighty-nine years of age, who faced death with a spirit of peaceful surrender. As she lay dying, she was lowly but audibly singing: "My soul's been born again." Her children, standing nearby at the time, later told the nurse of their mother's song. A few hours later the aged mother revived temporarily and the nurse asked her to sing the song. Once again, the elderly saint sang, "My soul's been born again." Hours later, she quietly bled to death internally. The doctor explained that she was worn out physically, but she was alive eternally.

A journey —At death we step through the doorway that separates this temporary world from the unseen, spiritual world. We are encouraged by the fact that Jesus invites us to step through the door with Him, just as He invited the thief on the cross. That thief did not understand what he was about to face in death, and beyond death, but he found satisfaction in Jesus' words: "Today shall thou be with me in paradise." We do not know very much about heaven, or about what eternity shall be like. But the primary thing which we do know about it is that we will be with Christ. Friends and loved ones have already stepped through it and we recognize that some day we too shall take that step. They are with Him face to face, and some day we shall be too. We do not have all the answers about where our departed loved ones are, but we have a connection with them through Christ. We know they are in His presence, and so we know that by looking to Him He becomes a connecting point. I have read stories about people who, knowing they were going to be separated, made a pact whereby they would each fasten their gaze upon the sun, or upon some star, at a stated time each day. This gave them the feeling that though they were out of sight of one another, their lines of sight would cross. As we lose loved ones, we need to remember that they will be viewing Christ from the world beyond, while we look to Him in this world.[9] How well I remember the words of a little six-year-old girl after the funeral of her grandfather. She had loved him dearly and so she made the request that when it came time for her to die, that she might be taken to the same hospital, and placed in the same room, so that when she died she would go

163

where her grandfather was. In a very childish way, she was expressing an inner hope shared by so many. Yet it does not matter in the least what our departure point is as we begin the journey of death. Christ is always there, wherever we are, to make the journey with us.

Although I believe that we shall know our loved ones, I do not believe it will occupy as primary a part of heaven as we so often make it. Being face to face with Christ will be the primary blessing of heaven. Knowing one another will always be secondary.

A falling asleep—Although the Bible teaches plainly that to be absent from this earthly life is to be consciously present with Christ, one of the most meaningful pictures of death is that of falling asleep. When the apostle Paul sought to console the Christians at Thessalonica who had lost loved ones, he spoke of their departed loved ones in terms of those who were asleep. The second death is spoken of as a time when men weep and wail as they see it approaching. In contrast, physical death for the Christian is pictured as a gentle falling asleep.

James Weldon Johnson has a beautiful poem entitled "Go Down Death" in which he pictures death as an angel of God. In the poem, God orders death to go down and find sister Caroline who is tired and weary, and to bring her to heaven. Peter Marshall, in a sermon entitled "Go Down Death," tells the story of a little boy who had an incurable illness. As the days passed, the little fellow gradually began to realize he would not live. One day he asked his mother quietly: "Mother, what is it like to die? Mother, does it hurt?" The mother, making some excuse, fled the room before her eyes filled with tears. Yet she realized she must answer the question. Later she returned to his room and said: "Kenneth, do you remember how you used to play so hard when you were a small boy, and that at night you would be too tired even to undress and get ready for bed? Do you remember that you would tumble into your mother's bed and fall asleep? That was not your bed; it was not where you belonged. In the morning you would wake up and find yourself in your own bed in your own room. Your father had come, while you slept, and with his big strong arms had carried you away." Then the mother continued, "Kenneth, death is just like that. We just wake up some morning and find ourselves in the other room—the room where we belong—because the Lord Jesus loved us." The little lad never asked the question about death again, and several weeks later he fell asleep just as his mother had told him.[10]

A beginning—As we face up to Christ, we recognize that death is never to be looked upon as an end, but as a beginning. Christ promised His disciples, and us (John 14), that He is preparing a place for us and that He shall return some day to lead us to it. The resurrection keeps the grave from being our final destination. The risen Lord assures us that death has indeed been defeated. Eternal life lies just beyond the doorway of death. If Christ is some day to return for us, then it changes all our values. We must never forget this. Most biographies begin with the birth of the person involved and relate the details of his life up to the moment of his death. There the story ends. Yet in a very real sense the story is just beginning. True biography is incomplete this side of eternity. Death merely marks the end of Part I and announces the coming of Part II. We hear again the words of Jesus: "I am the resurrection, and the life: he that believeth in me, though he were dead, yet shall he live" (John 11:25). Jesus admits we shall die, but He assures us it is the beginning of life eternal.

Because death is merely a beginning, we can face its coming with quiet assurance. During World War I, Rupert Brooke wrote a poem entitled "Safety." It contains a great message:

> Safe shall be my going.
> Secretly armed against all death's endeavor;
> Safe though all safety's lost;
> Safe where men fall;
> And if these poor limbs die, safest of all.[11]

I cannot leave this subject without saying something about death for the non-Christian. Everything that brings assurance to the Christian brings a sad message to the nonbeliever. The reality of a life to come where men inherit heaven or hell presents nothing but the prospects of fearful agony and utter loneliness for the nonbeliever. Better for him if the grave did end it all, but it doesn't. The fact that the nonbeliever does not fear death in this life is really beside the point. There is no indication that the rich farmer in Luke 12 feared death. Yet the words: "This night thy soul shall be required of thee," spell his utter doom. He lives in a world where nothing is going to be all right, for he lives in a world that will at last kill him. There is an old spiritual that goes like this: "We are going down the valley one by one, we are going toward the setting of the sun. . . ."

Henrik Ibsen, in his drama *Brand*, says: "Death is the rostrum of life."[12] Death has much to say to us about life. If we will listen to death, we shall find the proper perspective for life. If we will but heed the message of death, it will point us to the living Christ.

NOTES

1. R. Lofton Hudson, *Persons in Crisis* (Nashville: Broadman Press, 1969), p. 110.
2. Ibid., p. 111.
3. Paul Tournier, *The Whole Person in a Broken World* (New York: Harper & Row, Publishers, 1964), p. 23.
4. Helmut Thielicke, *I Believe: The Christian's Creed* (Philadelphia: Fortress Press, 1968), p. 136.
5. Ibid., p. 139.
6. Cf. E. Stanley Jones, *Christ and Human Suffering* (New York: Abingdon Press, 1961), p. 218.
7. Ibid., p. 209.
8. Thielicke, *I Believe,* p. 254.
9. Ibid., p. 147.
10. Charles Allen, *Life More Abundant* (Old Tappan, NJ: Fleming H. Revell, 1969), p. 146.
11. Rupert Brooke, "Safety," William Barclay, *The Letter to the Romans* (Edinburgh: St. Andrew Press, 1955), p. 11.
12. Hudson, *Persons in Crisis,* p. 115.

16

The Promises of Heaven

"And I saw a new heaven and a new earth" (Rev. 21:1).

A child awakens in the middle of the night from a bad dream and cries out amidst the surrounding darkness that threatens him. His mother turns on the light, takes him in her arms, and says reassuringly, "Don't cry, everything's going to be all right." This life situation is presented by Peter Berger in his book *A Rumor of Angels*, together with this question: "Is the mother lying to the child?"[1] Berger rightly concludes that unless there is a supernatural reality beyond the natural world, the mother is indeed lying because the mother and child live in a world that will eventually kill both of them.

Death forces every person to have a philosophy of life, to attempt to make some sense of existence, or to deny all sense of meaning, as the case may be. This places many in the category of the man who discovered he had been speaking prose all his life without knowing it. We each have an outlook on life, a philosophy.

Aristotle, in the *Physics* and the *Politics*, explained that we learn the nature of anything only as we study its *telos*, its final stage. The true worth of a block of marble is seen only in terms of the finished statue.[2] So our existence, this thing called life, cannot be ultimately understood apart from our final destiny. At this point the doctrine of eternity, of a heaven and hell, takes its proper importance. It is final destiny that determines life's values and meanings.

The Christian does not demand that every injustice be made right in this life. There is another life, another final and eternal episode to come. In an age of revolution and violence, so marked by the absence of religious faith, Victor Hugo's words become particularly relevant: "If you persuade Lazarus that there is no Abraham's bosom awaiting him, he will not lie at Dive's door, to be fed with his crumbs—he will make his way into the house and fling Dives out the window."

While critics of Christianity have often accused its proponents of enslaving the masses by the promise of "pie in the sky by 'n bye," some of the greatest tragedies of human existence have grown out of naturalist beliefs that have caused men to grasp for everything in the here and now, believing there is no tomorrow. Hitlers and Stalins can arise only from the ashes of such naturalism.

Faust sold his soul to the devil in exchange for earthly success and was later told by Mephistopheles that the value of everything was ultimately nothing. How true this is if your "everything" is composed of earthly dust. Such temporary treasures make doubly tragic the last words of Sir Walter Raleigh, written from his tower prison as a part of his unfinished *History of the World:* "O eloquent, just and mighty death! whom none could advise, thou hast done; and whom all the world hath flattered, thou only hast cast out of this world and despised. Thou hast drawne together all the farre stretched greatnesse, all the pride, crueltie and ambition of man, and covered it all over with these two narrow words: *Hic Jacet!*"[3]

James Denney observed that the thought of death is second only in scope to the thought of God. Yet because of God, death is not the end. There is a heaven.

On first thought, we would expect so great a concept as heaven to be elaborately described in the Bible. Yet such is not the case. When asked to define heaven, we feel our kinship to Augustine as he told of his struggle to define time: "If nobody asks me what time is, I know: if I want to explain it to anyone who asks me, I am at a loss."

Weatherhead explains Jesus' reticence to describe

heaven by likening such an attempt to trying to explain the beauty of a sunset to a man born blind.[4] Words are inadequate. Heaven is described in Scripture in terms of a place as secure and glorious as a city of gold, as peaceful as a garden, as radiant as the sun, and as victorious as a conquering army.

Needless to say, heaven must be thought of in terms of a new dimension which we cannot comprehend with human senses. Just as God is ever present beside us, in an unseen, spiritual way, so even our departed loved ones may be very near, though in another dimension of existence. Some anonymous poet voices this hope beautifully:

> Though I am dead, grieve not for me with tears,
>   Think not of death with sorrowing and fears,
> I am so near that every tear you shed
>   Touches and tortures me, though you think me dead . . .
> But when you laugh and sing in glad delight,
>   My soul is lifted upward to the Light:
> Laugh and be glad for all that Life is giving,
>   And I though dead will share your joy in Living.[5]

ETERNAL LIFE

It is the avowed purpose of God to bring His children to eternal life (John 3:16). As Christ walked among men, He affirmed: "I am come that they might have life, and that they might have it more abundantly" (John 10:10). The full life begins at the moment of conversion (John 5:24) but grows toward a final fullness in heaven. Jesus depicted the end of time in terms of a judgment at which time the righteous will enter into "life eternal" (Matt. 25:46).

Heaven is a place of survival, a place where life continues. Human personality and consciousness does not end at death. The soul is no longer housed in a physical body, but this does not mean the absence of form. There is a resurrection body, a body fitted for the new dimension of existence. It is a body related to the earthly body just as a planted seed is related to the new stalk—but they are not identical (I Cor. 15:37-39). One bears the image of the earthly; the other of the heavenly.

After the resurrection, Christ could appear and disappear. He could be touched (Luke 24:39), yet could go through locked doors. He was not easily recognized, but bore a resemblance to His earthly body. He even showed His wounds.

However, heaven is more than just a place of survival, for hell is also such a place. Heaven is marked by fullness of life. "Eternal life" is only secondarily marked by endlessness. Its primary characteristic is that of quality. Hence John's vision of heaven is that of a place not just where "there shall be no more death," but where there shall be "neither sorrow, nor crying, neither shall there be any more pain: for the former things are passed away" (Rev. 21:4).

Here is to be a quality life. In this context, and this context only, death loses its sting. A. H. Strong tells of two martyrs being led to the stake, one blind and one lame. Said one to the other as the fire was kindled, "Courage, brother! this fire will cure us both!"[6] Here God's alpha finds its omega. The first and the last, the beginning and the end join together in God's eternity.

The opposite of eternal life is not annihilation; it is the curse. All men are destined to live on, but only heaven is worthy of being described in terms of life. Lord Bacon once said, "Being, without well-being, is a curse, and the greater the being, the greater the curse."[7] Perhaps the most fearful aspect of hell is its utter meaninglessness—its utter separation from all purpose, from all good, and most of all, from God.

What a contrast is heaven's glory. A place of life! An elderly woman in a nursing home made the statement: "To live too long is a nuisance." Heaven will know no such loneliness or despair.

COMMUNION

Heaven is not some eternal crypt, but rather a place of

meaningful relationships. John sees it as a place where God pitches His tent with men and lives in their midst (Rev. 21:3) while they serve Him and glory in His presence (Rev. 22:3; 19:1).

To live in heaven is to be a part of a redeemed society. Good and evil will have been localized and separated: "And there shall in no wise enter into it anything that defileth, neither whatsoever worketh abomination, or maketh a lie" (Rev. 21:27).

Not least among heaven's joys will be that of reunion with loved ones. All kinds of problems can be raised by our finite minds as to how we can know one another, particularly babies who have died and others whose death came only after much disablement. This brings up the question of what age-appearance people will have in heaven. Will babies appear as their adult potential? Will the old have a body resembling that of their prime. All these questions must remain unanswered, but with the many evidences of E.S.P., and the premise that all our senses will be heightened in eternity, we need have no fear of not being able to recognize one another.

The most touching scene in the life of David Brainerd comes in his farewell to the young woman, Jerusha, whom he had planned to marry. She was the daughter of Jonathan Edwards and had sought to nurse Brainerd back to health but he was too far gone. His mission efforts to the Indians had destroyed his health and the dread tuberculosis would not be denied. To Jerusha, Brainerd said, "If I thought I should not see you, and be happy with you in another world, I could not bear to part with you. But we shall spend a happy eternity together."[8]

Because of heaven, the past becomes our treasure. Some poet has said, "What you have experienced, no power on earth can take from you."[9] Our departed loved ones become our treasure, but they do not remain in the past. Indeed, they are part of our eternal future toward which we are traveling. There are many documented accounts of patients who, in the process of dying, have verbally conversed with loved ones long since dead so as to indicate an unseen reunion being begun at the moment of death. Surely all of these cannot be explained away in terms of delirium. I have talked with patients living near death's precipice who affirmed they had seen departed loved ones beckoning to them.

ENDLESS GROWTH

Heaven is to be a place of activity and progress. Dante saw heaven as a place where there is nothing to do, a place you desire only in order to escape hell. But God is not static. His heaven will be a place where we can pursue interests and dreams in a way earth could not permit.

The Bible indicates there is to be a "new kind" of heaven and earth (Rev. 21:1). The words used indicate a renewal of the present earth, leading many to believe this earth to be the location of the eternal heaven. While this earth, cleansed by a final conflagration and renewed by the mighty power of God, may well be the home base of our eternal existence, I have a feeling that all the grandeur of the universe will be involved. I cannot believe that God created the myriad of galaxies for no reason. What more exciting future could there be than that of exploring the universe?

Heaven will be a place where man's hunger for knowledge can find fulfillment. There we will no longer have to be content to see through a glass darkly. We can see face to face. There the many unanswered questions of human suffering will be made clear. Viktor Frankl uses the illustration of an ape being used to develop a poliomyelitis serum and explains that the ape can never understand why he is being punctured again and again. The ape can see no meaning to his pain because his limited intelligence shuts him out of the world of meaning.[10] So heaven is a new dimension, not only of existence, but of understanding and knowledge.

Even the concept of rewards should not be viewed as static. We will not be given some final trophy which we set on the shelf and dust occasionally. The idea of rewards should not be viewed in terms of the holiest being given larger houses in which to live. I believe rewards will be tied up with our spiritual capacity to enjoy heaven. Just as part of our reward will be the joy of presenting before God a life of faithful service, so a part of our reward will be determined by how much capacity we have for spiritual blessings. Heaven is a place where we shall be "filled with all the fulness of God" (Eph. 3:19). But all vessels are not the same size. During periods of drought on the farm, I used to haul water for the livestock. I had a truck loaded with barrels and cans of varying sizes. I filled each one, but not with the same amount.

The faithful servant who has spent much time in self-denial and prayer, in works of compassion and witness, will have a greater spiritual capacity for enjoying heaven than will the one who was saved by the skin of his teeth (I Cor. 3:15). Yet each will have the joy of growth and progress. The fact that heaven is pictured as a place of perfection does not rule out the idea of growth. Jesus was born in perfection. All He did was perfect, yet He grew in understanding throughout His life. The rosebud may be perfect, but it develops and opens. Weatherhead likens heaven to a good concert for a man musically inclined. He feels that this is where he belongs. A man not musically inclined would be completely bored.[11] So heaven is a place for those who have been made spiritually alive through faith in Christ. The unredeemed, the spiritually insensitive, would not be happy in heaven even if allowed to enter.

In light of heaven's glory, death for the Christian is rather insignificant. Since life and progress goes on, what great difference does it make if our address is earthly or heavenly? This means that death does not defeat God's purpose. The Christian who lies dying, and asks, "Will I get better?" can be answered with a truthful Yes.[12] He will indeed get better as soon as death grants his release.

This helps us at the point of whether or not we should grieve for the dead. Grief is only natural. We cannot keep from missing our loved ones and friends. But we do need to recognize, as Weatherhead points out, that the Christian stance looks upon a departed loved one in much the same attitude as if the loved one had merely moved far away to another continent. We miss him, but we know we shall see him again, and that in the meantime he is alive and involved in fulfilling God's purpose.[13] Weatherhead, a clergyman with considerable clinical experience, explains that he has never found anyone dying in mental unhappiness. Often there is fear and dread as death approaches, but when the moment arrives, if there is consciousness, the patient gives indication of an extremely happy experience. When the physician to the royal family lay dying, he said, "If I had strength to hold a pen I would tell mankind what a wonderful thing it is to die."[14]

No wonder Jesus likened the kingdom of heaven to a pearl of great price for which a man willingly gives everything he owns. Incidentally, the "kingdom of heaven" and the "kingdom of God" are used interchangeably in Scripture. Each has to do with the reign and authority of God. Heaven is a place where this reign is full and complete.

Through Jesus Christ, the reign of heaven, the authority of God, has dipped into the human story. To surrender in faith to Christ is to yield to the divine rule of God in the here and now, to taste briefly and partially of its peace, and to await its ultimate fullness beyond this earthly sojourn. Hence Jesus gave priority to man's need of surrendering to God's rule: "But seek ye first the kingdom of God, and his righteousness; and all these things shall be added unto you" (Matt. 6:33).

The kingdom of heaven is more important than the many things to which we give ourselves for it puts us in league with God's future. Paul was a citizen of Rome, but he took greater pride in the fact that he was a citizen of heaven (Phil. 4:20).

It was an ancient custom in some of the early centers of Christianity to give new converts observing their first Lord's Supper a cup of milk and honey in addition to the bread and wine as a reminder of the future promise of God's kingdom.[15] In the words of Bunyan, "the milk and honey is beyond the wilderness." We need to remember this when it seems that the wilderness is about to destroy us.

And now back to the question with which we began: Is the mother lying to the child when she soothingly says, "Everything is going to be all right"? Indeed not! Everything can be all right because there is a heavenly Father and an eternal heaven, and we shall someday see them both when the divine glory of which we have seen but brief glimpses breaks upon us in all its fullness. From the world's point of view, this victory will occur in a most unexpected way—by our death! This makes of every pain a divine promise, not merely of death's approach, but of Life's entrance.

> Sunset and evening star,
>   And one clear call for me!
> And may there be no moaning of the bar,
>   When I put out to sea,
>
> But such a tide as moving seems asleep,
>   Too full for sound and foam,
> When that which drew from out the boundless deep
>   Turns again home.
>
> Twilight and evening bell,
>   And after that the dark!
> And may there be no sadness of farewell,
>   When I embark;
>
> For tho' from out our bourne of Time and Place
>   The flood may bear me far,
> I hope to see my Pilot face to face
>   When I have crost the bar.[16]

Notes

1. Peter L. Berger, *A Rumor of Angels* (Garden City, NJ: Doubleday and Company, Inc., 1969), pp. 68-70.
2. J. S. Whale, *Christian Doctrine* (Cambridge: at the University Press, 1961), p. 171.
3. Ibid., pp. 172-73.
4. Leslie Weatherhead, *Life Begins at Death* (Nashville: Abingdon Press, 1969), pp. 11-12.
5. Ibid., p. 8.
6. A. H. Strong, *Systematic Theology* (Philadelphia: The Judson Press, 1907), Three Volumes in One, p. 1022.
7. Ibid., p. 1035.
8. J. M. Sherwood, *The Life and Character of David Brainerd* (no publication data), p. 340.
9. Viktor Frankl, *Man's Search for Meaning* (New York: Washington Square Press, Inc., 1963), p. 131.
10. Ibid., p. 187.
11. Weatherhead, *Life Begins at Death*, p. 55.
12. Ibid., pp. 87-93.
13. Ibid., pp. 18-19.
14. Ibid., p. 18.
15. *Cambridge Ancient History,* XII, p. 527.
16. Alfred Lord Tennyson, "Crossing the Bar," in *Masterpieces of Religious Verse,* ed. James Dalson Morrison (New York: Harper & Brothers Publishers, 1948), poem 1991.